CONFEDERATES COURAGEOUS

The Story of the Confederate Submarine

H.L. HUNLEY

BY GERALD F. TEASTER

ISBN 0-9744556-0-1

Published by Junior History Press
Box 157, Summerville, SC 29484-0157.

First Printing - March, 2004
Second Printing - April, 2004
Third Printing - April, 2005

Printed in the U.S.A. by
Morris Publishing
3212 East Highway 30
Kearney, NE 68847
1-800-650-7888

Foreword

This book tells the story of the Confederate submarine *Hunley*. It became the world's first successful submarine when it sank the Federal ship *USS Housatonic* outside of the harbor of Charleston, South Carolina during the Civil War. The sinking was a bitter victory because the *Hunley* and its crew were lost. The submarine was lost for 131 years until it was found in 1995. The sub was raised in August, 2000 and is now undergoing examination and preservation at the former Charleston Naval Shipyard.

The first part of the story was told in my book "*The Confederate Submarine H.L. Hunley*" published by Junior History Press in 1989. The discovery, recovery and newly found facts about the submarine led to writing this present book "*Confederates Courageous*." This book incorporates the material in the 1989 book and includes details of how the sub was found, how it is being preserved and new discoveries about it. Many things have been found out about the *Hunley* that are different from what was previously thought and described in the 1989 book. This new book details these differences.

The material in this book relating to the finding, recovery and preservation of the sub comes from two major sources. The first is the Friends of the *Hunley* organization and their press releases. This group is in charge of the efforts to preserve the submarine. The second source is the news coverage of the *Charleston Post and Courier* newspaper. The *Post and Courier* did a superb job in dealing with all aspects of the *Hunley* story.

Illustrations and photographs, unless otherwise noted, are by the author.

This book includes a Glossary to identify the major places, terms and individuals in the story of the *Hunley*. Items listed in the Glossary are shown in bold type the first time that they are used in the following chapters.

The story of the *Hunley* is far from over. Many discoveries still await the scientists involved in the project. Many controversies must be resolved before the final *Hunley* story is told.

Gerald F. Teaster,
January, 2004

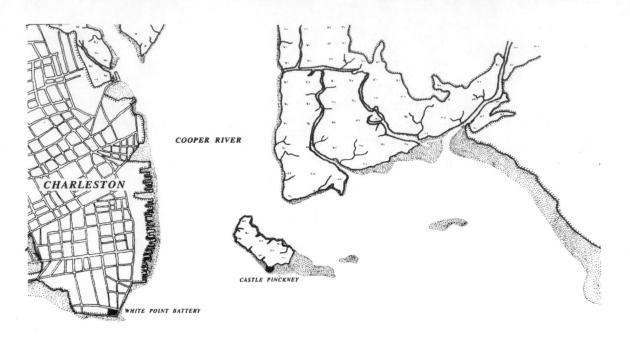

COOPER RIVER

CHARLESTON

CASTLE PINCKNEY

WHITE POINT BATTERY

ASHLEY RIVER

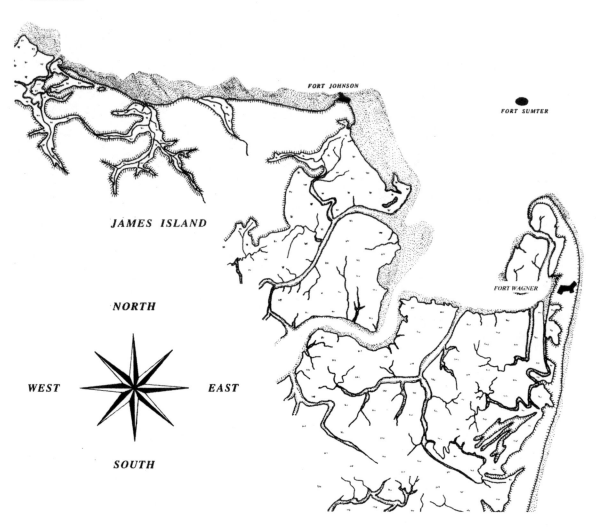

FORT JOHNSON

FORT SUMTER

JAMES ISLAND

FORT WAGNER

NORTH

WEST   EAST

SOUTH

MOUNT PLEASANT

ISLE OF PALMS

BATTERY MARSHALL

SULLIVAN'S ISLAND

FORT MOULTRIE

CONTENTS

HOUSATONIC SUNK

HUNLEY FOUND

The Civil War and the Blockade

Introduction

Submarines are a very important part of today's United States' Navy. They provide a way for carrying men and weapons under the ocean without being seen from other ships or airplanes. During wars, submarines are used to attack other ships and targets on land. Modern submarines are huge and carry sophisticated rockets and torpedoes, but the first successful use of a submarine was in the United States Civil War. This submarine was called the *Hunley* after one of its builders. It was tiny when compared to the submarines of today. This is the story of that first successful submarine, the men who built her, and the battle that she fought.

On April 12, 1861, the Civil War, also called the War Between the States, began in the harbor of **Charleston, South Carolina**. The first shot of the war was fired at the Federal (Northern) troops stationed on the island fort, called **Fort Sumter**, in the mouth of Charleston harbor. This city, where the war began, is also where the *Hunley* marked her place in history.

Charleston, South Carolina was a major seaport for the South at the time of the Civil War. Ships from all over the world would come to Charleston to deliver their goods. During the war, this was an important way for the South to get guns and supplies.

The Federal Government tried to stop the trading ships from coming into Charleston and other Southern ports. They set up a blockade by stationing large war ships across the mouth of the harbor to prevent ships from going in or out of Charleston.

Many small, fast ships were used by the South to slip between the large Northern warships, usually at night. These fast boats were called blockade runners. Blockade runners helped to bring supplies into Charleston but were too small to carry much on each trip. It was very expensive and dangerous to depend on blockade runners to bring in all the supplies the South needed. The South had to find a way to break through the blockade of its ports. Several new and different weapons of war were developed by the South in an effort to break the blockade. Of these, the most successful and enduring has been the submarine.

Building the *Hunley*

Chapter 1

The *Hunley* was intended from the beginning to be a submarine. The submarine was not all together a new idea. A one-man model, *The Turtle,* had been tried unsuccessfully by David Bushnell to sink British ships in the Revolutionary War.

Three men built the South's submarines during the Civil War. They were **Captain J. R. McClintock** and **Captain H. L. Hunley** of the Confederate States Army and **Mr. Baxter Watson**, a civilian engineer. The Confederate government supplied the money for the first ship.

Their first submarine was started in New Orleans in 1862. The city fell into Northern (or Federal) hands before the ship was finished. The builders sank the partly finished boat in Lake Pontchartrain to keep it from being captured and went to Mobile, Alabama.

A second boat was built in the Park and Lyons machine shop in Mobile. This boat was twenty-five feet long and tapered at each end. Its makers named it the ***Fish Torpedo Boat.*** Upon completion it was towed out to make an attack on blockaders around Mobile. This boat also met with failure when it sank in the waters off the coast of Mobile. Fortunately, no lives were lost.

After the sinking of the boat at Mobile, the Confederate Government no longer believed in the project and stopped supplying money. Captain Hunley, however, was convinced that the idea was sound. He persuaded the other two men to start a third boat which he paid for with his own money.

This third boat is the main character of our story. The little ship was named *H. L. Hunley* after the man who believed in it so much.

The recovery and inspection of this vessel, beginning in August, 2000, has changed many of the ideas about how it was made and worked.

It was of unusual construction. The men began with a steam boiler about three and one half feet in diameter and twenty-five feet long. They split this into two parts. They jacked these sections apart and added an iron strip down both sides. This gave the boat an oval shape that was about four feet high and three and one half feet across.

Next, they built a tapered section on each end. This gave the boat an overall length of about forty feet. At each end of the boat, within the tapered section, they installed a tank that could be filled with water.

These were the ballast tanks. Their purpose was to make the boat heavy enough to actually submerge. Each of the tanks was fitted with a hand pump so that water could be pumped out of the tanks. When water was pumped out, the boat would rise to the top.

The next item of construction was the drive or propulsion system. This was a **crankshaft** running almost the length of the boat with seven separate cranking stations so it could be turned by seven men.

The end of the crank rod was equipped with a chain gear sprocket similar to that on a bicycle. A chain connected this sprocket with another one that was attached to the end of the propeller shaft. The propeller shaft protruded into the **aft ballast tank** and then through to the outside of the boat. Just behind the propeller shaft sprocket, there was a circular, iron flywheel about three feet in diameter. The purpose of this heavy flywheel was to help store the energy from cranking and smooth out the cranking forces applied to the propeller.

The boat was fitted with a row of cast iron weights or **ballast** along the bottom on the outside. In case of an emergency, this iron could be dropped by turning bolts that stuck through the hull, allowing the sub to rise back to the surface.

The boat could be steered left and right by a hinged rod mechanism located just behind the bulkhead for the **forward** ballast tank. This rod was connected to the **rudder** on the aft end, or back end, of the boat by a mechanism located under the crew's bench. All previous descriptions of the *Hunley* had mistakenly said that the boat was steered by a wheel located over the captain's head.

The *Hunley* could dive by opening a valve and letting sea water fill the ballast. A set of crude **diving planes**, sticking out the side of the boat, was also provided for up and down motion. A mercury **manometer**, or pressure gage, was mounted inside to show the depth.

Two small hatches were installed on the top of the boat to allow the crew to get in and out. Each of these had small glass viewing ports.

The crew consisted of six men and one officer to turn the crank and one senior officer to command and act as "look out" through the **hatch** port.

The weapon for the submarine was a **torpedo**. It carried ninety pounds (some sources say 135 pounds) of black powder explosive. Several methods had been considered to detonate the torpedo.

The first idea was to float the explosive on a line behind the submarine. At the time of attack, the submarine would dive

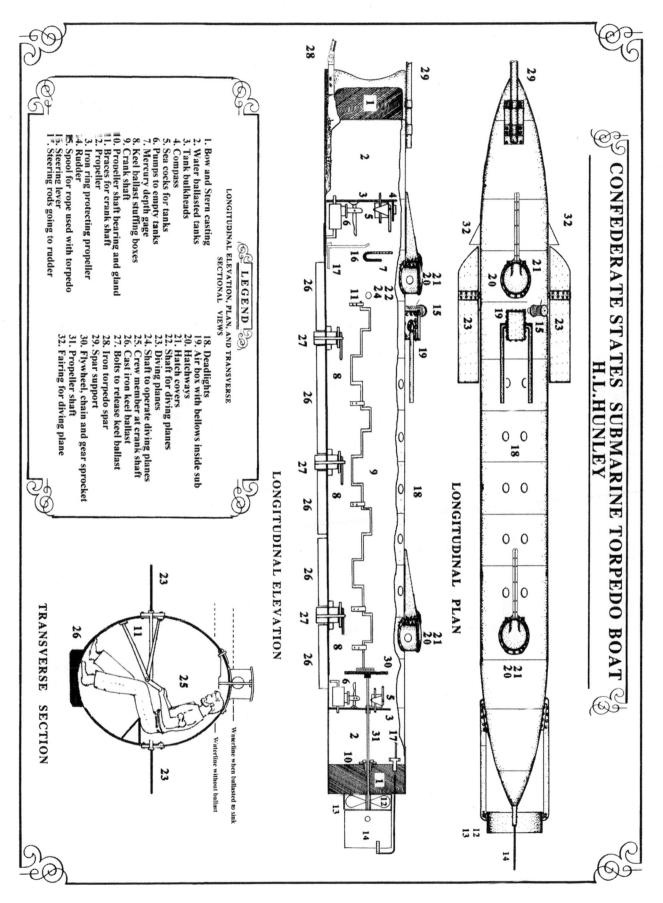

CONFEDERATE STATES SUBMARINE TORPEDO BOAT
H.L. HUNLEY

LONGITUDINAL PLAN

LONGITUDINAL ELEVATION

TRANSVERSE SECTION

Waterline when ballasted to sink

Waterline without ballast

LEGEND

LONGITUDINAL ELEVATION, PLAN, AND TRANSVERSE SECTIONAL VIEWS

1. Bow and Stern casting
2. Water ballasted tanks
3. Tank bulkheads
4. Compass
5. Sea cocks for tanks
6. Pumps to empty tanks
7. Mercury depth gage
8. Keel ballast stuffing boxes
9. Crank shaft
10. Propeller shaft bearing and gland
11. Braces for crank shaft
12. Propeller
13. Iron ring protecting propeller
14. Rudder
15. Steering lever
16. Spool for rope used with torpedo
17. Steering rods going to rudder
18. Deadlights
19. Air box with bellows inside sub
20. Hatchways
21. Hatch covers
22. Shaft for diving planes
23. Diving planes
24. Shaft to operate diving planes
25. Crew member at crank shaft
26. Cast iron keel ballast
27. Bolts to release keel ballast
28. Iron torpedo spar
29. Spar support
30. Flywheel, chain and gear sprocket
31. Propeller shaft
32. Fairing for diving plane

under the target and the torpedo would strike. In actual practice, the torpedo would not behave. It would not stay at the end of the tow rope. It almost sank the submarine itself.

In another method, the torpedo was mounted on a wooden pole about twenty-two feet long fastened to the **bow** or front of the submarine. In an attack, the submarine would silently approach the ship and ram the torpedo against its side. Until the lost *Hunley* was found, this was the way that historians thought the ***Housatonic*** had been sunk.

A third method had been tried during the early testing of the sub. The torpedo had also been attached to a long wooden pole. The torpedo was slipped onto the pole so that it could come off easily. The torpedo itself was made with a sharp spike, somewhat like a nail, so that it would stick into the wood hull of an enemy ship. A long rope was fastened to the exploding mechanism of the torpedo and tied onto a spool on the submarine. During the attack the sub would go forward and stick the torpedo and spike into the target ship. Once the torpedo was stuck in place, the crew would reverse their cranking and back the sub away from the ship. The sub going backwards would tighten the rope and this would explode the torpedo.

The recovered *Hunley* showed that a variation of the last method was actually used. However, instead of a long wooden pole mounted on top of the sub, an iron **boom** attached to the bottom of the front of the sub was used. This iron boom was hinged where it attached to the sub and could be set at different angles. This allowed it to be adjusted to hit the ship at different depths under the surface.

It is believed that the successful torpedo and firing mechanism was designed by Mr. E.C. Singer, a nephew of the inventor of the sewing machine

The submarine was finally finished and tested. It worked basically as planned. The Confederate Government decided that the submarine could best be used to break the blockade at Charleston. The boat was very carefully loaded on two railway flat cars and taken slowly over the route from Mobile to Charleston.

The *Hunley* arrived in Charleston about August 15, 1863.

Diving With The *Hunley*

Chapter 2

After its arrival in Charleston, the *Hunley* got its first crew made up of all volunteers. The Captain was **Lt. John Payne**. The crew began working to perfect its operating procedure.

Let's imagine that we could accompany the crew while they made a dive. The crew steps down off the dock onto the deck or top of the submarine. The deck is almost under water even though both dive tanks are empty. One half of the crew enters the back hatch and the other half enters the front. This is necessary because of the cramped space inside.

The crew members take their place at the crank stations. The Captain lights a candle. This candle serves two purposes. First, it provides much needed light. Without it, the inside of the sub is very dark. The small overhead deadlights provide minimal light. The candle also serves as a warning when the oxygen supply in the air is getting to a low level. The candle will flicker and go out when the amount of oxygen in the air gets low.

The officers tighten down the hatch covers very tightly. The lines are released from the dock. As the crew begins to crank, the submarine starts to move slowly. The crew has found that at top speed, the submarine will do about 4 miles per hour. This is not very fast, since it is about as fast as a man walks on land.

The Captain steers the boat and operates the forward tank. The second officer operates the **stern** tank and turns on the crank with the rest of the crew.

The Captain gives the order to dive. He opens a valve on the forward tank. This allows sea water to enter the submarine to fill the tank. The tank is open at the top. The captain must be careful to close the valve soon enough or the tank could overflow into the crew section of the boat. If this happens, the boat could sink all the way to the bottom.

While the Captain fills the forward tank, the second officer fills the stern tank. The tanks are filled until the top of the deck is about three inches under water. The Captain can tell when this happens by looking out the viewing ports in the hatch. When the right level is reached, the valves to the tanks are closed.

The temperature and humidity in the boat increase rapidly so it is very uncomfortable. While the crew cranks, the captain steers. He has a lever mounted close to the bulkhead in front of him that is linked to the rudder at the stern of the ship.

The Captain can tell his depth by using the mercury gage mounted on the side of the boat.

The Captain can make the boat rise or sink using the diving planes. These are flat pieces of metal sticking out on both sides of the boat. There is a lever at the Captain's position so that he can operate these planes. When he moves the lever in one direction, the boat rises and when he moves the lever in the other direction, the boat settles. The diving planes only work when the boat is moving forward.

The Captain gives the order to surface. He sets the diving planes for rise. The crew continues cranking. The Captain begins to pump the water out of the forward tank. At the same time the second officer is pumping out the stern tank. Each of the tanks has a small hand pump for this purpose. The pumping operation is slow and tedious.

With the tanks empty, the boat stays on the surface. The Captain and second officer open the hatches and a draft of cool, clean air fills the boat. The dive has been successful.

A descendent of the *Hunley*, the USS *Salt Lake City* (SS N716), prepares to go alongside the sub tender *USS Frank Cable* (AS40) in Apra Harbor in Guam . The *Salt Lake City* is nine times longer than the *Hunley*. (US Navy Photograph)

Disaster and Misfortune

Chapter 3

The *Hunley* had only been in Charleston a short while when a series of misfortunes began.

Lieutenant Payne and his crew were preparing for a mission. The *Hunley* was just leaving the pier. All of the crew except Lt. Payne had already boarded. As Lt. Payne started to enter the open hatch, a passing boat threw up a swell or caused some disturbance that completely swamped the *Hunley*. First it turned on its side and then the open hatches allowed enough water in to completely sink it. Lt. Payne was washed clear and escaped, but five of the men inside were trapped. The *Hunley* had claimed the first of its many victims.

The Confederate authorities sent for Capt. Horace Hunley. They believed the accidents were caused by the crew's inexperience with the new submarine.

Capt. Hunley was one of the original builders of the boat and had previously volunteered to operate the boat. He came to Charleston from Mobile accompanied by a volunteer crew.

The boat was raised, cleaned, and inspected and its equipment repaired. It was then turned over to Capt. Hunley. His crew made several successful dives.

On October 15, 1863, while making practice dives under the Confederate vessel ***Indian Chief***, the *Hunley* went down and failed to surface. When raised and opened, the submarine presented a horrible sight. Mr. **W. A. Alexander** of New Or-

leans had been scheduled to be aboard with this crew, however, at the last minute he could not join them. This is how he described the recovery of the *Hunley:*

"The boat when found was lying on the bottom at an angle of 35 degrees, the bow deep in the mud. The hold down bolts of each cover had been removed. When the hatch covers were lifted, considerable air and gas escaped. Captain Hunley's body was found with his head in the forward hatch-way. His right hand was on top of his head. He had been trying, it would seem, to raise the hatch cover. In his left hand was a candle that had never been lighted. The sea-cock (or valve) was wide open. **Mr. Parks'** body was found with his head in the after hatch-way, but the pressure was too great. The other bodies were floating in the water. Hunley and Parks were undoubtedly suffocated, the others drowned. The bolts that held the iron keel ballast had been partly turned but not sufficient to release it."

From this, Alexander was able to determine what had happened. Hunley had attempted to flood his tanks and set his diving planes for dive before he lit his candle. Evidently, the boat sank quicker than he planned. The candle could not be lighted before the boat sank below the glass panes in the hatch. This put the boat in total darkness and he could not find the valve in the darkness to stop the flooding.

The members of this crew were all buried in Charleston. Their graves can be found on Kings Circle in Charleston's **Magnolia Cemetery**.

The loss of this crew put the list of the *Hunley* casualties at 13. Historians dispute the total number of times the *Hunley* was sunk and the number of men killed.

In March, 2000, members of the first *Hunley* crew were also buried in Magnolia Cemetery. This crew was moved from another location in Charleston to Magnolia.

The last *Hunley* crew, recovered from the submarine, joined them in Magnolia in April, 2004. These men were the last Confederates of the Civil War to be buried. Many ceremonies and a formal military funeral were held. People from all over the United States and even foreign countries came to Charleston for the funeral.

The Confederate Section of Magnolia Cemetery decorated for Confederate Memorial Day.

The graves of Horace Hunley and his crew in Magnolia Cemetery.

HERE RESTS THE CREW OF THE
CONFEDERATE SUBMARINE *Hunley*
DIED ON OCTOBER 15, 1863 WHEN
MAKING A PRACTICE DIVE IN THE HARBOR

HORACE L. HUNLEY
ROBERT BROCKBANK
JOSEPH PATTERSON
THOMAS W. PARK
CHARLES McHUGH
HENRY BEARD
JOHN MARSHALL
CHARLES L. SPRAGUE

Enlargement of inscription on monument.

Practicing For The Attack

Chapter 4

After the drowning of Capt. Hunley's crew, **General Beauregard** issued the order that the *Hunley* was not to be used as a submerged boat. The boat would have to operate on the surface in the same manner as the steam torpedo boat, ***David.***

Again, the *Hunley* was raised and refitted. Another crew was obtained and practice for the attack continued. A first hand account by a member of this crew, Mr. W. A. Alexander, tells us the story in his own words:

"We soon had the boat refitted and in good shape, reported to **General Jordan**, Chief of Staff, that the boat was ready again for service, and asked for a crew. After many refusals and much dissuasion, General Beauregard finally assented to our going aboard the CSN receiving ship, *Indian Chief,* then lying in the river, and secure volunteers for a crew, strictly enjoining upon us, however, that a full history of the boat in the past, of its having been lost three times and drowning twenty-three men in Charleston, and full explanation of the hazardous nature of the service required of them was to be given to each man. This was done, a crew shipped, and after a little practice in the river we were ordered to moor the boat off **Battery Marshall**, on Sullivan's Island. Quarters were given us at Mount Pleasant, seven miles from Battery Marshall. On account of **chain booms** having been put around the *Iron-sides* and the **monitors** in Charleston harbor to keep us off these vessels, we had to turn our attention to the fleet outside. The nearest vessel, which we understood to be the United States frigate **Wabash**, was about twelve miles off, and she was our objective point from this time on.

In comparatively smooth water and light the *Hunley* could make four miles an hour, but in rough water the speed was much slower. It was winter, therefore necessary that we go out with the **ebb** and come in with the flood tide, a fair wind and dark moon. This latter was essential to success, as our experience had fully demonstrated the necessity of occasionally coming to the surface, slightly lifting the after hatch cover, and letting in a little air. On several occasions we came to the surface for air, opened the cover and heard the men in the Federal **picket boats** talking and singing. Our daily route, whenever possible, was about as follows;

Leave Mount Pleasant about 1 p.m., walk seven miles to Battery Marshall on the beach (this exposed us to fire, but it was the best walking), take the boat out and practice the crew for two hours in the **back bay**. **Dixon** and myself would then stretch out on the beach with the compass between us and get the bearings of the nearest vessel as she took her position for the night; ship up the torpedo on the boom, and when dark, go out, steering for that vessel, proceed until the condition of the men, sea, tide, wind, moon, and daylight compelled our return to the dock; unship the torpedo, put it under guard at Battery Marshall, walk back to quarters at Mount Pleasant and cook breakfast.

During the months of November and December 1863, through January and the early part of February, 1864, the wind held contrary, making it difficult with our limited power, to make much headway. During this time we went out on an average of four nights a week, but on account of the weather, and considering the physical condition of the men to propel the boat back again. often, after going out six or seven miles, we would have to return. This we always found a task, and many times it taxed our utmost exertions to keep from drifting out to sea, daylight often breaking while we were yet in range. This experience, also our desire to know, in case we struck a vessel (circumstances required our keeping below the surface), suggested that while in safe water we make the experiment to find out how long it was possible to stay under water without coming to the surface for air and not injure the crew.

It was agreed to by all hands to sink and let the boat rest on the bottom, in the back bay, off Battery Marshall, each man to make equal physical exertion in turning the propeller. It was also agreed that if anyone in the boat felt that he must come to the surface for air, and he gave the word 'up', we would at once bring the boat to the surface.

It was usual, when practicing in the bay, that the banks would be lined with soldiers. One evening, after alternately diving and rising many times, Dixon and myself and several of the crew compared watches, noted the time and sank for the test. In twenty-five minutes after I had closed the after manhead (hatch) and excluded the outer air the candle would not burn. Dixon forward and myself aft, turned on the propeller cranks as hard as we could. In comparing our individual experience afterwards, the experience of one was found to have been the experience of all. Each man had determined that he would not be the first to say 'up!' Not a word was said, except the occasional 'How is it?' between Dixon and myself, until word 'up' came from all nine. We started the pumps. Dixon's worked all right, but I soon realized that my pump was not throwing. From experience I guessed the cause of the failure, took

off the cap of the pump, lifted the valve and drew out some seaweed that had choked it.

During the time it took to do this, the boat was considerably by the stern. Thick darkness prevailed. All hands had already endured what they thought was the utmost limit. Some of the crew almost lost control of themselves. It was a terrible few minutes, 'better imagined than described.' We soon had the boat to the surface and the manhead (hatch) opened. Fresh air! What an experience! Well, the sun was shining when we went down, the beach lined with soldiers. It was not quite dark, with one solitary soldier gazing on the spot where he had seen the boat before going down the last time.

He did not see the boat until he saw me standing on the hatch combing, calling to him to stand by to take the line. A light was struck and the time taken. We had been on the bottom two hours and thirty-five minutes. The candles ceased to burn in twenty-five minutes after we went down, showing that we had remained under water two hours and ten minutes after the candle went *out*.

The soldier informed us that we had been given up for lost, that a message had been sent to General Beauregard at Charleston that the torpedo boat had been lost that evening off Battery Marshall with all hands.

We got back to the quarters at Mount Pleasant that night, went over early next morning to the City (Charleston), and reported to General Beauregard the facts of the affair. They were all glad to see us.

After making a full report of our experience, **General Rains,** of General Beauregard's staff, who was present, expressed some doubt of our having stayed under water two hours and ten minutes after the candle went out. Not that any of us wanted to go through the same experience again, but we did our best to get him to come over to Sullivan's Island and witness a demonstration of the fact but without avail. We continued to go out as often as the weather permitted, hoping against hope, each time taking greater risks of getting back. On the last of January we interviewed the Charleston **pilots** again, and they gave it as their opinion that the wind would hold in the same quarter for several weeks."

His recollections were printed in the *Mobile Daily Herald* newspaper on July 2, 1902. His account, written many years after the War, does not always agree with other accounts or some of the details as found on the recovered submarine.

Mr. Alexander was ordered to report to Mobile, Alabama to help develop a new type of gun. He was therefore to miss the next part of the *Hunley's* experience.

Breach Inlet as it appears today.

These houses now sit about where Battery Marshall was located.

The Federal ship, *USS Housatonic*, from a painting by R. G. Skerrett done in 1902.
(US Navy Illustration)

The *USS Housatonic*

Chapter 5

The night of February 17, 1864, was cold. The sea was calm, but there was bright moonlight. As they had done in the past, Lt. Dixon and his crew prepared to take the *Hunley* on patrol. The men in the crew this night besides Lt. Dixon were A. Becker, C. Carlson, F. Collins, J. Ridgeway, C. Simkins, J. Wick, and a Mr. Miller. The trip started as many in the past had,

but this one was destined to be very different.

The men busied themselves with getting the submarine ready to go. The most important and dangerous part of getting ready was mounting the torpedo on the boom. After every trip, the torpedo was removed and stored under armed guard at Battery Marshall. The torpedo had to be refitted to the boom before each trip. This was sometimes a difficult task. The torpedo weighed more than one hundred pounds and contained ninety pounds of black powder. One

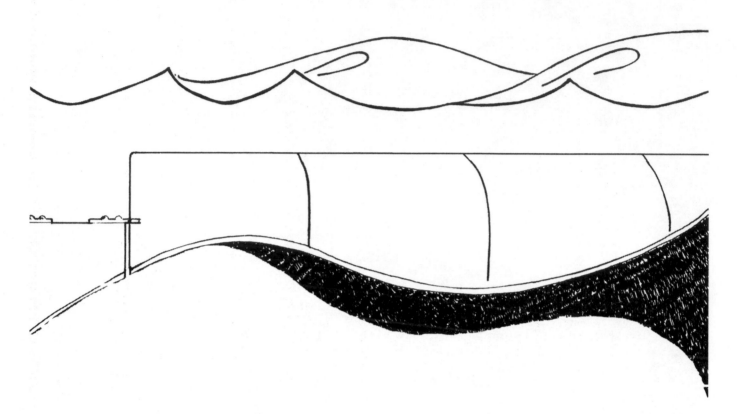

slip at the wrong time could be disastrous. The torpedo was picked up very carefully and fastened to the end of the boom. If the sea was rough, this was an awkward task. On this night, with a calm sea, mounting the torpedo went smoothly. After it was in place, the rope from the spool on the sub was fastened to the firing mechanism. The *Hunley* was now armed and ready to sail.

The crew climbed into the submarine through the forward and aft hatches. Lt. Dixon motioned to the soldiers on the pier to cast off the mooring ropes. Dixon se-cured his hatch as the men slowly began to turn the crank. The boat creeped away from the pier into the water of the Back Bay. As usual, since Beauregard's order, the boat was to operate on the surface. Still, most of the boat was underwater.

The inside of the boat was very cold at first but turning the crank warmed the men quickly. The temperature and humidity in-side the submarine increased rapidly.

Every man was busy with his task even though all were uncomfortable. The cramped, muggy, barely lit submarine was

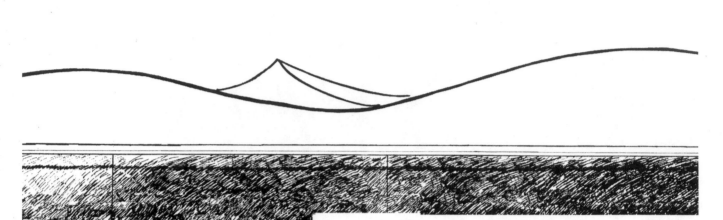

not a pleasant place to work.

Still every man gave his maximum effort. They knew that if they were successful in sinking a ship, it would be a great day for the Confederacy. Each knew that food and supplies in the South were getting more and more scarce. Maybe, if they were lucky, the blockade could be broken.

The men cranked and the boat made its way slowly along the tidal creek behind Sullivan's Island. Lt. Dixon turned the boat to the right to begin its passage through Breach Inlet. Breach Inlet is a very narrow strip of water separating Sullivan's Island from the Isle of Palms. The current there is very rough and the boat shook and rolled as it made its way cautiously through the Inlet.

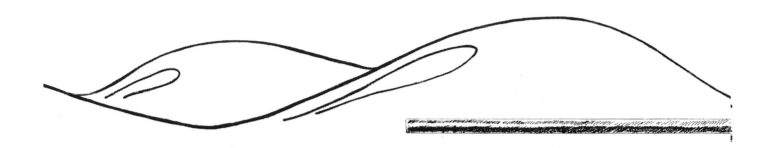

Lt. Dixon steered toward the open sea. Through the little glass porthole in the hatch, he could see the moonlight on the ocean. He hoped that the moonlight would not allow them to be seen. Like all of the men, Lt. Dixon knew how vulnerable they really were. Basically, they were underwater in an old steam boiler with a bomb fastened to it. To make matters worse the bomb, or torpedo, was only twenty feet or so from the inside of the submarine. They were on their way in this contraption to attack some of the most powerful ships in the world. It was a dangerous job.

The men cranked mostly without talking. Still it was noisy inside the submarine. The crank clanked inside its supports as it was turned. The sound of the waves slapping against the top of the subma-

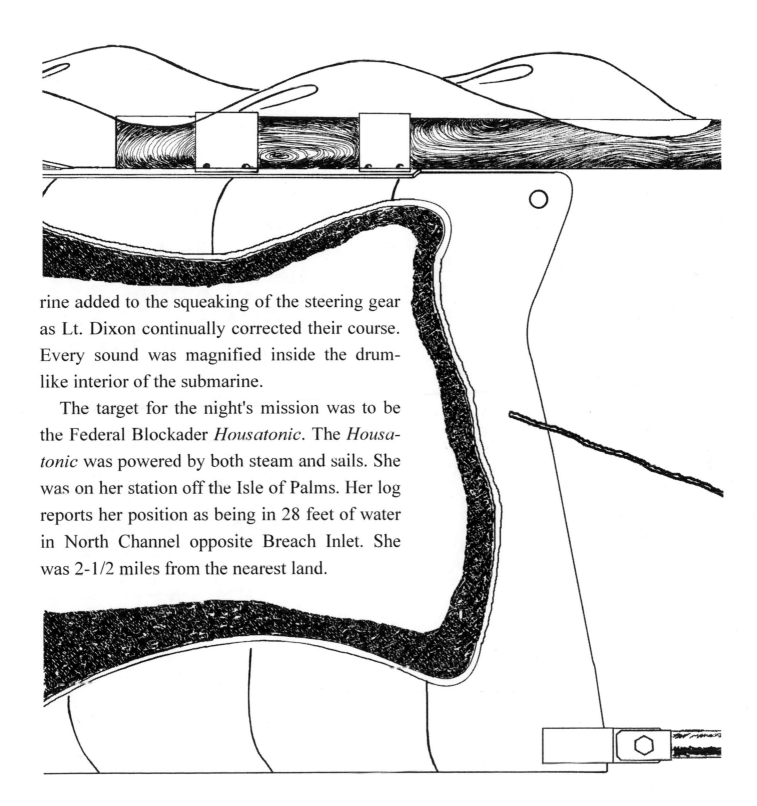

rine added to the squeaking of the steering gear as Lt. Dixon continually corrected their course. Every sound was magnified inside the drum-like interior of the submarine.

The target for the night's mission was to be the Federal Blockader *Housatonic*. The *Housatonic* was powered by both steam and sails. She was on her station off the Isle of Palms. Her log reports her position as being in 28 feet of water in North Channel opposite Breach Inlet. She was 2-1/2 miles from the nearest land.

Lt. Dixon of the *Hunley* could make out the outline of the *Housatonic*. He steered directly toward her, his crew straining at their cranks. The humidity in the submarine was overwhelming. The walls of the submarine were dripping wet with condensed water and their clothes were soaked. Still, every man was intensely excited. The moment had come! They were actually making an attack. Closer and closer they came. They had not been seen. Surprise was still on their side. They got to within a few feet of the *Housatonic* before they were seen. Pistol shots rang out from the officers on board the *Housatonic*. The crew of the *Hunley* could hear the pistol bullets ricochet off the metal top. It was too late now to stop the

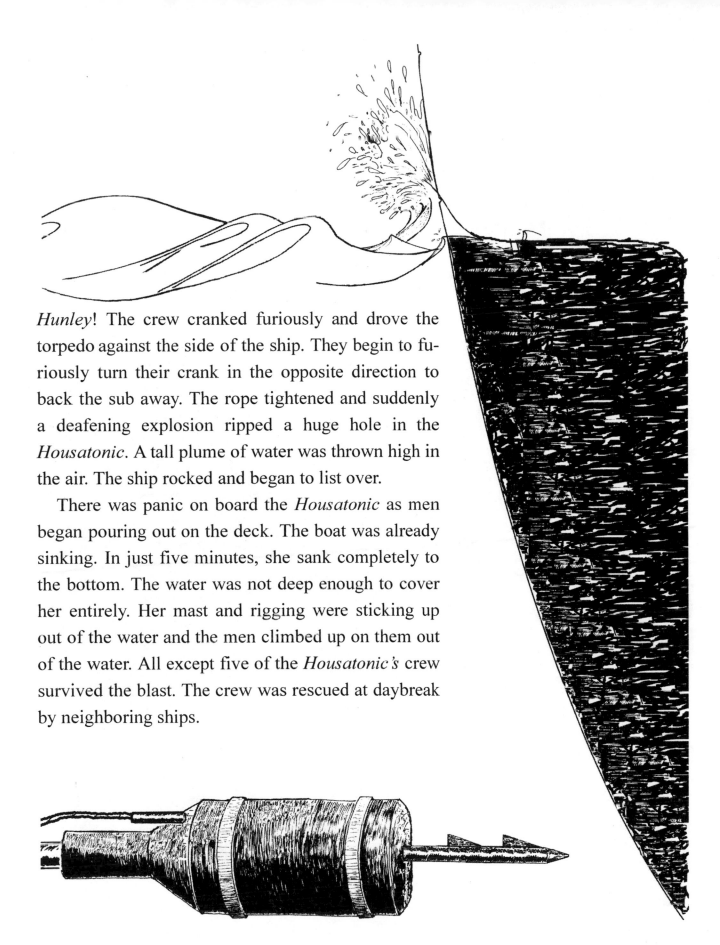

Hunley! The crew cranked furiously and drove the torpedo against the side of the ship. They begin to furiously turn their crank in the opposite direction to back the sub away. The rope tightened and suddenly a deafening explosion ripped a huge hole in the *Housatonic*. A tall plume of water was thrown high in the air. The ship rocked and began to list over.

There was panic on board the *Housatonic* as men began pouring out on the deck. The boat was already sinking. In just five minutes, she sank completely to the bottom. The water was not deep enough to cover her entirely. Her mast and rigging were sticking up out of the water and the men climbed up on them out of the water. All except five of the *Housatonic's* crew survived the blast. The crew was rescued at daybreak by neighboring ships.

The *Hunley* itself is another story. It was lost with its entire crew for 131 years. No one knows to this day exactly what happened. Scientists studying the recovered submarine hope to answer that question. One guess was that the boat was moving forward at its fastest speed. The *Housatonic*, in trying to get away, began to move backwards. This motion could have brought the two boats together with the *Hunley* going partly up inside the *Housatonic*. However, we now know that this was not the case. The *Hunley* was discovered at quite a distance from where the *Housatonic* sank. The *Hunley* was able to maneuver for a short period of time after the attack and explosion.

Regardless of the cause, the *Hunley* was lost. Word of the sinking of the *Housatonic* quickly reached Charleston. There was

much rejoicing and talk of breaking the blockade. Observers reported seeing a blue light after the explosion. This was the signal the *Hunley* was supposed to send if they were successful. The Confederate authorities hoped the *Hunley* had survived and would still be heard from. As time went on their hopes dimmed. Finally, it was admitted that the *Hunley* and its crew had been lost.

The *Hunley* was the first submarine to sink a ship but the South paid a heavy price for it. The *Hunley* killed at least 21 Confederate and 5 Federal sailors.

It is important to keep in mind the actual size of the *Hunley*. It was about the same size as one of the modern day Trident missiles. A present day nuclear Trident submarine is equipped with twenty four missiles of this size.

The Lost *Hunley* is Found

Chapter 6

The *Hunley* was lost on the night of February 17, 1864. For 131 years, what had happened to the little boat was a mystery. Many attempts were made to find it.

Some people thought that the wreckage of the *Hunley* had been destroyed when the harbor was dredged in the late 1800's.

In 1995, the author, **Clive Cussler**, financed and led a search to find the *Hunley*. Cussler is the founder of the **National Underwater & Marine Agency (NUMA).** This organization searches for lost ships and so far has found more than 60 shipwrecks.

In May, 1995, the Cussler expedition's use of high technology search equipment and persistence paid off. **Ralph Wilbanks**, **Wes Hall** and **Ralph Pecorelli** were divers hired by Cussler. They found the *Hunley* off Charleston Harbor under three feet of mud in water that was less than 30 feet deep.

The submarine was not in the location where it had sunk the *USS Housatonic* in 1864. Evidently, it had survived the explosion and was trying to make its way home by going into Charleston Harbor.

The wreck was verified to be the *Hunley*. Cussler refused to release the exact location of the find until he was satisfied that the submarine would be raised and preserved properly. Even though the sub was found in May of 1995, Cussler did not divulge the exact wreck location to the Navy's Historical Center until November of 1995.

Who Owns the *Hunley*?

The find of the lost submarine was the focus of much local, national, and worldwide attention. The discovered submarine was the property of the United States Government because they acquired all the property and assets of the defeated Confederate Government in 1865.

The state of South Carolina wanted the submarine because it was located in South Carolina waters and had played such an important part in the state's history. The SC state legislature established a *Hunley* **Commission** to look after South Carolina's interest in the *Hunley* and to plan for its future. State **Senator Glenn McConnell** was named Chairman. Senator McConnell and the Commission have been instrumental in safeguarding the *Hunley* and making plans for its raising, preservation and display.

The question of ownership of the submarine was settled in an agreement between the state and the Federal Government that was signed in August, 1996. Under this agreement, the submarine will stay in SC forever. The United States retains title to the recovered submarine but South Carolina has custody.

Plans were made to raise and preserve the submarine and display it in a new section of the Charleston Museum. A non-profit organization known as **"The Friends of the *Hunley*"** is raising the money for the project. Originally, it was expected that the sub would be raised in the year 2001. However, the recovery date was moved up and the submarine was successfully raised on Tuesday, August 8, 2000. There was a huge celebration in Charleston when the *Hunley* was brought home.

Estimates for the cost of the *Hunley* project range from 17 million to 20 million dollars.

The *Hunley* lies on the bottom about 25 feet down awaiting recovery. Each end is marked by a small buoy. The nearest buoy is connected to the submarine bow.

The platform crane *Karlissa B* that was used to recover the *Hunley*.

The *Hunley* is Recovered

Chapter 7

Recovering the *Hunley* and transporting it back into Charleston was an expensive and complex operation. By May, 2000 a recovery team was put together that included the National Park Service, the U.S. Navy and the state of South Carolina. The company in charge of the *Hunley* lift was **Oceaneering International Inc.,** a com-pany with a long record of deep sea recov-eries.

Steps in the Recovery

At a press conference in May, 2000, a representative of Oceaneering Interna-tional described how the recovery would be done. The steps would be:

1. Divers will vacuum away sand around the sub. In this area,- considered part of the official Hunley Battlefield, ar-chaeologists will search for any pieces of the sub that may have broken away in the attack, such as the spar that carried the powder charge. This was expected to take about three weeks to complete.

2. Salvage team divers will spend the next couple of weeks setting the foundation for the steel lift truss that will carry the sub's weight when it is lifted.

The sub will rise to the surface in a hammock-like sling and a bed of foam-filled pillows. "The foam will assume the shape of the Hunley," the representative said.

3. Once secure on the deck of the recovery barge, the sub will be towed to its conservation lab at the former Charleston Navy Base, where it will be submerged in a protective tank of cold water. The interior of the sub will be excavated inside the tank, where the Hunley will remain for five to ten years.

(The recovery procedure went as the representative described except that various problems were encountered and the entire procedure took longer than first expected.)

Recovery Begins

The actual recovery operation began on Saturday, May 13, when the 180-foot-long work boat **Marks Tide** left its mooring at the former Charleston Navy Base and went to the *Hunley* wreck site, 4 1/2 miles off Sullivan's Island. It carried divers, archaeologists, and engineers.

Hunley Commission Chairman, Glenn McConnell, announced that The National Geographic Society had agreed to make a documentary of the recovery, including filming the difficult underwater segments. NGS would pay $200,000 toward the recovery costs for the film rights.

Divers from the *Marks Tide* quickly began the task of vacuuming the sand from around the *Hunley*. They soon found small pieces of wood and coal buried near the sub that project archeologists say may have come from the *Hunley*'s victim, the *USS Housatonic*. The two conning towers on the sub were among the first parts of the sub to be exposed by the vacuuming.

Divers were able to work in the 30-foot-deep water about four hours at a time using breathing equipment. The water temperature was about 78 degrees and visibility was near zero. One diver was quoted as saying "It's pitch black. You can't see a hand in front of your face but you gradually get used to it."

As the vacuuming progressed, corrosion and preservation specialists began testing the hull of the sub to see exactly what kind of shape it was in and to determine how well it would do when removed from the ocean. They were working to test the corrosion rate of the material in an attempt to determine the overall integrity of the iron sub's hull.

Safety Zone is Established

Federal and State officials were con-

The barge to be used to transport the *Hunley* awaits its priceless cargo.

cerned with the safety of the project divers and the possibility of someone removing items from the wreck. The S. C. Department of Natural Resources Law Enforcement Marine Patrol, the U. S. Coast Guard, and the Department of Natural Resources (DNR) established an exclusion zone around the project's location off Sullivan's Island. The exclusion zone was marked with eight large yellow buoys, and onlookers had to stay outside of this marked area.

Discoveries

As the divers cleared away more sand and silt from the submarine, they found that the *Hunley*'s rudder was broken off and missing. The rudder is a flat plate mounted behind the submarine's propeller and is used to steer the boat to the right or left. The propeller was in place and intact but a part of its surrounding protective ring was also missing. There was an object laying beside the sub that could possibly be the rudder but could not be identified until more sand was removed.

The removal of more sand uncovered a small bolt on the sub's bow that archeologist suspected may have secured the spar - the long pole that carried the sub's black-powder charge. They also discovered a small place in the bow where something like a spar pole might have been attached according to the Project Manager, **Dr. Robert Neyland**. He described the object as "a big bolt that sticks out about 3 or 4 inches from the hull."

The Spar is Found

The last week in May, divers and archeologists answered one of the sub's biggest mysteries. They found the boom, or spar, that was used to carry the sub's torpedo with 90 pounds of gunpowder in the attack . The 17-foot-long pole was buried in the sediment. It is made of iron, not wood as was previously believed. The spar was still attached to the submarine. At first the spar was believed bolted on and mounted about midway up the sub's bow - not right on top of it, as shown in various pictures and as depicted on the *Hunley* replica outside the Charleston Museum. Later, more detailed examination revealed that the spar was attached more towards the bottom of the bow rather than in the middle.

On the same day that the spar was found, the divers also discovered a large, 3-foot long hole in the aft part of the submarine.

Molds are Made

While excavation work proceeded, archachaeologists began making molds of the *Hunley's* hull structure.   They wrapped sections of the submarine with a special fiberglass tape to create a mold to show the sub's actual shape. The completed molds will enable a more accurate weight and volume estimate of the water and sand trapped inside the submarine. Amazingly, molds of the hull show it was about 4 feet tall, indicating that the men inside probably had to crouch severely as they cranked the propeller. This is much smaller than was expected. Civil War era accounts say that the crew portion of the sub was five feet high.

New Recovery Date is Announced

The work of removing the sand and silt around the sub was going so well by the end of May, that plans were made to move up the date on which the *Hunley* would be recovered by about three weeks. On June 2, State Sen. Glenn McConnell, chairman of the *Hunley* Commission, announced that, assuming no surprises, the new estimated lift date for the *Hunley* would be June 27.

Bacteria is Studied

The first week in June, biologists from the National Park Service and Medical University of South Carolina visited the *Hunley* site. Their mission was to sample and study the various types of bacteria that had been drawn to the wreck and to try to determine which ones were feeding on the iron of the submarine. The study of the bacteria associated with the *Hunley* will continue after the sub is recovered.

Spar is Removed

Also the first week of June saw the removal of the iron spar from the submarine. The bolt holding the spar was cut and a wrench was put on the square head of the bolt. The bolt snapped into two pieces but both pieces were recovered. The bolt was described as about one inch in diameter. The loosened spar was moved a short distance away from the sub but was kept under water until it could be removed properly for preservation.

During this operation, as mentioned before, it was found that the spar was attached closer to the bottom of the bow than the top. One archaeologist involved said the spar might be as low as 4 inches from the bottom of the bow.

Major Problem Threatens Project

On Friday, June 9, the entire *Hunley* recovery project hit a very big obstacle. It was determined that the large crane intended to raise the *Hunley* did not perform well in the open ocean. The barge and crane donated by Detyens Shipyard could not handle the offshore waves; it pitched too much in the 5-foot seas. Because of the importance of the crane to the entire operation, the project officials decided to delay the recovery until a proper crane could be located and brought to the site. Originally, it was believed that the crane problem would only cause a delay of a few days, but actually it delayed the recovery by almost six weeks.

More Discoveries

Divers continued their work and kept making new discoveries. A small, hand sized piece of iron was found halfway down the **port** side, between the rear conning tower and the propeller. It probably was intended to act as a trim tab to help stabilize the submarine. It is likely that a similar one will be found on the **starboard** side. No mention of these tabs had been found in researching the submarine.

Spar is Recovered

On June 13, the first significant part of the *Hunley* was brought to the surface and returned to Charleston. The iron torpedo spar was fastened to a steel beam and brought to the surface and then brought aboard the *Marks Tide*. From there it was transferred to a Charleston Harbor Pilot boat and taken to the preservation facility in North Charleston.

Work on Project Stops

The search was still continuing for a new crane to lift the submarine but with little success. By the week of June 21, underwater work on the submarine was coming to a halt pending the availability of a recovery crane. By June 24, the work had stopped. The submarine was covered with sandbags to protect it until the recovery effort could resume. The work boat *Marks Tide* loosed its mooring and returned to Charleston. The recovery effort was on hold until the proper crane could be found and brought to the site.

Still More Discoveries

However, just before the dive work stopped, another discovery was made. The divers found the cutwater that had broken off of the sub's rear conning tower. The cutwater is a triangular piece of iron that helps make a smoother flow of water over and around the tower as the sub moves through the water. There is a similar cutwater for the forward tower that was still in place.

Even though work had stopped at the dive site, it was still going on at the preservation center. Investigators found that the iron torpedo spar was bent a few degrees to the right. They believe that this bend was caused as the *Hunley* hit the hull of the *Housatonic* at the time of the explosion.

Crane Problem is Solved

A solution to the crane problem was not found until the second week in July. A suitable crane was found in the Dominican Republic. However, it was registered under the name of a foreign country, Belize. US law forbids a foreign-flagged vessel from salvaging a U.S. ship if an American salvage company is available to do the same work. Amid considerable political maneuvering the owners of the crane, Titan Marine, had it re-flagged and registered as a United States vessel.

The crane that was found was the 175-foot-long ***Karlissa B***. It was a vessel that can withstand almost any ocean turbulence. It has six extendable legs that can lift the barge's work platform high above the choppy surf, just like an offshore oil rig. The crane on the vessel can lift a load of 600 tons. The *Karlissa B* originally was built by the US Army Corps of Engineers. During the Korean War, it was used as a pier for ships that had no harbor available. After being declared surplus for military use, it was modified for private service and cut up into two salvage vessels. The other vessel, her sister ship, is the *Karlissa A*.

According to *Hunley* Commission Chairman, state Sen. Glenn McConnell, the Recovery Project saved a great deal of money by using the *Karlissa B*. Her owners, Titan Marine, made the crane available for the project for a fee of about $294,000. The next closest offer was around $600,000, he said.

The marine barge and crane, towed by a tug boat, left the Dominican Republic on July 13, bound for Charleston. It completed the 1,200 mile trip with no major problems and arrived on July 21.

The *Karlissa B* lowers its hook to start the recovery process.

Work Resumes at Site

Once it became apparent that the crane problem was solved, work resumed at the wreck site. Divers cleaned out the sand that had filled the excavation and removed the sandbags that had been placed to protect the sub temporarily .

Once in Charleston, the *Karlissa B* was outfitted with gear needed to support the *Hunley* raising. On Monday, July 24, it was towed to the *Hunley* site. Once over the wreck, the *Karlissa B's* six legs were pushed into the ocean floor. The work deck was then "jacked up" high above the sea where it will be free of any rough wave ac-

tion and allow the work platform to stay steady and dry. The platform was locked in place one foot above the high tide line.

Once the *Karlissa B* was in place, work proceeded rapidly. The next day, Tuesday, July 25, the two large, cylindrical pilings were put into place, one at each end of the submarine. These pilings provide a place for the lift truss to sit while the sub is being prepared for lifting. The truss will support the lifting straps, as they make a cradle for raising the boat.

On Wednesday, July 26, the truss itself was lowered into its position sitting on the pilings. The divers then began the task of clearing sand and sediment to secure each of the 32 lift straps that would hold the boat as it is brought to the surface. Before each strap is slid under the sub a clear path must be made for it through the sand and sediment. The divers also installed foam filled inflatable pillows on each sling so that the submarine would not move as it is lifted. They wanted to lift the boat at the exact angle it was sitting.

Air Pipes (Snorkels) Found

While work was progressing with the straps, another hole, about 12 inches in diameter, was found in the sub, low on the starboard bow. They also made another major discovery about the sub. The two missing snorkels, or air pipes, were found on the bottom to the sub's starboard side. The longer of the two pieces is about 4 feet long. The air pipes were used to bring outside air into the sub through the **air box** that was on top of the sub. In actual use on the sub it was found that the air pipes were too small in diameter to work properly.

New Official Recovery Date

On Tuesday, August 1, the official recovery date was announced. The sub would be raised in one week on August 8. Eighteen of the thirty two lift straps were said to be in place and work was going smoothly.

Rudder Found

On Thursday, August 3, the last missing part of the *Hunley* was found. The rudder was found covered by sand and silt under the stern of the sub. It was brought to the surface. As of this date, 27 of the 32 lifting straps were in place.

Conservation Lab Named

Also on this date, a ceremony was held to name the $2.8 million conservation lab at the former Charleston Naval Shipyard in honor of **Warren Lasch**, chairman of Friends of the *Hunley*.

By Saturday, August 4, all but one of the lifting straps were in place. The *Hunley* was hanging off the bottom in its lifting cradle of straps. All sand and sediment was removed from around the boat and water could flow under and around it.

Route for *Hunley* Barge

On Sunday, August 6, the route for the *Hunley* barge up to the **Lasch Conservation Center** was announced. The route was chosen so that the public could have a view of the sub as it passed. The *Hunley* barge was to travel up the harbor in the regular shipping channel past Forts Moultrie and Sumter, then break off toward the Battery, past Waterfront Park and the Maritime Center. It was then to swing back to the Mount Pleasant side of the harbor, passing Patriot's Point.

The Submarine is Raised

Tuesday, August 8, 2000, brought worldwide news attention to Charleston to see the *Hunley* raised from the ocean floor.

As dawn broke, the crane *Karlissa B* loomed over the wreck site. Moored close to it was the barge that would transport the recovered submarine to the Conservation Center. Between the barge and the crane, there were two small yellow buoys about the size of beach balls. Those were the marker buoys for the *Hunley*. One was tied to the bow and the other the stern. Only about 25 feet down from these buoys, the *Hunley*, and its crew, were waiting.

It slowly became daylight. Boats of all sizes were gathering to watch the event. One of the biggest was a huge barge that was being positioned by a tug to help shelter the lifting area from the wind and currents. There were other tugs to help move the barge that would carry the *Hunley* back to land. There was a large boat for the news media and another large boat chartered by the Friends of the *Hunley* for public officials and dignitaries. Then Governor of South Carolina, Jim Hodges, was on the boat as well as former Governor Jim Edwards. There were many general pleasure boats but there was also a shrimp boat anchored with its outrigger booms extended to both sides. Finally, in an unusual comparison to the bigger boats, there was a single kayak paddling along followed by

Diver makes last minute inspection to cables connected to submarine lifting cradle.

The *Hunley* surfaces again .

three or four jet skis.

The crane lowered divers into the water and then lowered its main cable and hook. Suspended from the hook was the rigging for attaching to the lifting truss and cradle that held the submarine. The divers made the connection and the crane began to slowly reel in its cable. The top of the truss emerged and then, at about 8:35 AM the *Hunley* broke the surface. After 136 years it was once again in daylight. Boat whistles and sirens blew, people yelled and clapped and some cried.

The cradle with its fragile cargo was raised and slowly placed on the pitching barge. The submarine was smaller in diameter than expected. It was also much more streamlined than Civil War era paintings and descriptions had depicted. The excitement of actually seeing the submarine was tempered with the reality that it was a very small coffin for what was then thought to be nine men.

Looking at the bow of *Hunley* as it is being lifted to put on barge.

Transporting the *Hunley*

The cradle was finally secured and the supporting tug boats took the barge. The barge was accompanied by a large group of boats as it started its trip to bring the *Hunley* home. There were thousands of people at Fort Moultrie and the Battery waiting to catch a glimpse of the submarine. Flags at Fort Sumter and Fort Moultrie were at half mast in honor of the event.

The barge and its parade of boats were not able to keep to its publicized route because of shallow water. It was not able to pass close to Patriot's Point and the aircraft carrier *Yorktown*, where thousands of people waited to see the sub. The memorial ceremony scheduled for the *Yorktown* still took place. Civil War re-enactors gave the passing *Hunley* a cannon salute with volley after volley. Nine women, dressed in black, and representing the crew's families dropped flowers into the Cooper River.

The barge and its submarine passed on up the Cooper River. The procession brought traffic to a stop on the Cooper River Bridges. People stopped and aban-

Hunley just after being lowered onto barge.

Mourners and re-enactors honor the *Hunley* as it passes the *USS Yorktown.*

Hunley on barge makes its way up the Cooper River.

doned their cars to look over the rail of the bridge to see the *Hunley* far below. A short distance up the Cooper, the *Hunley* passed Magnolia Cemetery, the resting place for the first two crews killed on the boat. In the spring of 2004, the remains of the last crew joined their comrades in Magnolia.

End of Trip

The last stop for the sub was the Warren Lasch Conservation Center on the former Charleston Naval Base. An honor guard of re-enactors escorted the boat, being carried by a crane, from Pier Juliet to the building. The boat was brought into the building and lowered to the floor. The big door was shut and now the *Hunley* was inside and out of the weather. Seeing the boat, up close, in the confines of the building, made it chillingly real. Inside that small boat, brave and determined men had met a violent and almost indescribable death. Now, they were home.

The truss cradle and the *Hunley* were lowered into a large tank where the boat will spend up to seven years being preserved and having remains of the crew and other artifacts removed. Four clergymen blessed the vessel and a re-enactor bugler played Taps. The crew's long ordeal was over.

Finding the Truth

Chapter 8

In August, 2000, the submarine was placed in a 55,000 gallon chilled water tank in the laboratory. Chilled water minimizes bacteria and corrosion activity and protects and stabilizes the waterlogged submarine. The chilled water will begin the process of desalination of the submarine's metal parts while the sub is under going examination and preservation. The temperature of the water is maintained at 46 degrees F.

A team of scientists were assembled to conduct the examination and to begin the preservation process. Dr. Robert Neyland, Branch Head of Underwater Archaeology for the Naval Historical Center, is in charge of the entire project. **Maria Jacobsen**, an archaeologist from Texas A&M University, led the excavation of the *Hunley's* interior. **Paul Mardikian**, from the Sorbonne University Conservation Program in Paris is in charge of the conservation. Other specialists were brought in as the project progressed.

There was great public interest in seeing the *Hunley*. However, public viewing of the sub was not possible for a few weeks. Public viewing of the sub started on Saturday, October 14, 2000, and continued for

The submarine being brought into the Lasch Center.

Hunley is lowered into chilled water tank in Lasch Center.

several weekends. There was an enormous demand for the tickets to the tour. The web site offering the tickets was swamped with over two million hits when they went on sale. Public tours continued until the excavation of the sub began in early 2001.

Before the excavation started, the submarine was very accurately measured. This was done by laser scanning the entire boat. Scientists scanned the complete exterior before cleaning or removing accumulated concretion. The result was a diagram and pictorial model of the sub accurate to within about 1/16 of an inch. This information was used to plan the openings for the removal of the sub's contents.

Activities in the year, 2001

The scientists investigating the submarine began excavating the inside of the submarine on January 22, 2001. At that time, high frequency sonar scans of the sub showed that artifacts also existed inside the silt that filled the boat. Many of the artifacts were in the forward end of the submarine leading the scientists to think it sank bow first.

Deciding how to remove the contents of the submarine required careful study. The scientists wanted to get inside the boat with the least damage to the vessel. They decided to drill out the rivets holding some of the iron panels in place. Once this was done, alternating panels on the top half of the sub could be removed. This would allow the contents to be taken out. However, before this was started, some material was removed through an existing tear in the rear part of the boat. It was not known, in the beginning, whether or not any traces of the crew would be found. It was possible for the public to watch the excavation on wide screen televisions at the Lasch Center where the work was being done.

By the middle of February, efforts were underway to drill out and remove rivets holding some of the iron panels in place. After about a week, they had successfully removed one of the three hull plates to allow excavation of the sub's interior. A second and third panel followed over the next several days. Each panel had almost 100 rivets holding them in place. Scientists were surprised to find that the rivets were countersunk to make them flush with the sub's hull. This decreased the water resistance on the sub as it moved through the water and made it a little faster. A method very similar to this is used to rivet the parts of a modern airplane. The first hull plate removed was 33 inches in width, 64 inches in length, and 3/8 of an inch thick.

By the middle of March, the three hull plates were removed to allow access to the sub's interior and excavation had started. In the beginning, only silt containing seashells was found. Testing indicated that the sediment had a low oxygen content raising hope that the artifacts might be well preserved. Evidence obtained from the sediments above the sub indicated to the scientists that the vessel was completely buried within 15 to 20 years following the sink-

The Warren Lasch Center where the *Hunley* is undergoing examination and preservation.

ing.

In March, April and May the scientists made many discoveries. Also by May, several long held ideas about the sub were found to be wrong. These are discussed in detail in Chapter 9.

The first items found were two brass uniform buttons that were identified as being from the uniform of a soldier in an artillery unit from Alabama.

A board that was either part of a shelf or a seat was found along with a corked glass bottle and another wooden shelf.

A small portion of a leather belt was discovered from the mid-section of the submarine.

A small patch of textile fabric, about the size of a half-dollar and more buttons were found.

The handle for the hand pump in the stern section and the hand crank appeared.

The first evidence of human remains was discovered in March and by the end of April, remains of eight of the nine anticipated crewmen had been found. This included the skull and a nearly complete skeleton that was located aft in the area where one of the sub's officers would have operated the aft ballast tank. The most amazing discovery is that there was still brain tissue preserved in the skulls that had been uncovered. By the end of May, the remains of the final crewman had been found in the forward part of the sub. They were believed to be that of Lt. Dixon, the sub's commander.

One item found appeared to be a bellows that may have been used to increase air flow in and out of the air box.

Other items included pieces of cloth uniforms, buttons, a leather shoe, a wooden tobacco pipe, a short pencil, tin canteens, a candle and holder, and a two-sided, fine toothed comb, typical of the Civil War period.

Scientists also found the sole of a shoe or boot in the sediment near the remains. Another shoe had been previously found and was removed.

Two folding knives were discovered but were heavily concreted.

Scientists also recovered a "slouch" hat that belonged to one of the crew. A "slouch" hat is a wide-brimmed military hat, common in the Civil War era. The hat is dark in color and extremely fragile.

The scientists found what may be the steering rods for the sub. They were located beneath the bench that the crew sat on. This is not in the location shown on W.A. Alexander's historical sketches of the sub.

A mystery item was found. This was an identification tag for a Union soldier from Connecticut that was thought to be killed during an attack on Battery Wagner on Morris Island.

Also by the end of May, a *Hunley* legend was verified. The story of Dixon's gold coin was proven to be true. The *Hunley* scientists found the legendary coin. It is an 1860 U.S. $20 eagle gold piece. The coin was supposed to have been given to Lt. Dixon by his fiancé Queenie Bennett of Mobile, Alabama. Dixon was carrying the coin in his pocket when his unit, the 21st Alabama Infantry, was involved in the battle of Shiloh in April, 1862. Dixon was shot, but the bullet that hit him struck the coin in his pocket. The coin was deformed and Dixon was left with a limp. The story was told that he always carried the coin with him afterwards. This was confirmed when the bent coin was recovered from the area of Dixon's remains. The coin was not corroded and almost as bright as when the sub sank. The coin was engraved on the back with:

Shiloh
April 6, 1862
My life Preserver
G.E.D.
(G.E.D. was for George E. Dixon)

A lantern that may have been used to signal the success of the sub's mission and an open-ended iron wrench were found close to Lt. Dixon.

After this discovery, further excavations were stopped until the fall of 2001. During this time, the tours of the sub were again conducted and were very popular.

Final excavation of the *Hunley* started in October after being halted over the summer. Approximately 80% of the sub had been previously cleared of silt but some areas remained covered. One major point of interest was the space under the crew's wooden bench. There was speculation that if a log book was kept of the submarine's operation, this is where it might be found.

The excavation in the fall of 2001 made other exciting discoveries.

No more human remains were found. It was concluded that the *Hunley* definitely only had a crew of eight men. Past accounts all said that there were nine men in the crew. However, the remains of only eight were onboard. Investigation of the remains show that the crew ranged in age from 19 to their early 40's.

The wooden box that originally held the sub's compass was found in November. The box, about 10 inches by 10 inches by 6 inches, had no top or bottom and was made of a soft wood. Attached to the box was a gimbal, or pivoting ring, that would have allowed the compass to swing freely and stabilize at a level position. When the box was removed, archaeologists found the actual compass. It had come to rest against the forward bulkhead and, with time, got concreted to the bulkhead. The glass pane of the compass is in place and not broken. The compass itself was in very poor condition.

The propeller driving system has been found to be more complex than originally thought. It was believed that the crank was fastened directly to the propeller. However, the drive has been found to have a set of gear-sprockets, a drive chain and a flywheel. This feature gave a mechanical advantage to the drive system and increased the turning torque that the crew could give to the propeller. The flywheel stored some of the energy of the crew cranking and helped smooth out the torque applied to the propeller.

A section of iron chain concreted to the bottom of the hull was found near the propulsion gears. It was probably a spare section of chain in case the installed one broke. A metal file about 13 inches long and one inch wide was also found.

It was confirmed that the sub's ballast tanks were open at the top. The W.A. Alexander account of the submarine described the open tanks. The aft bulkhead is located about a foot-and-a-half behind the rear conning tower and it is open to the after ballast tank. The iron wall stops almost a foot from the ceiling of the hull. This open tank top would allow water from the ballast tank to pour into the *Hunley's* central compartment if the sub were tipped or lost an even keel.

The scientists have found three of the bolts that were used to release the sub's lead keel ballast in an emergency.

More details were found about the crew bench mounted along the portside wall of the sub. It was found to be made of three wooden sections, supported by a number of brackets.

Beneath that bench, workers uncovered another artillery uniform button and four more canteens. Some of the mechanism for the steering also was located under the crew's bench.

While the excavation was continuing, investigative work was also being done in other areas. A photograph, long thought to be that of Lt. Dixon, was found to be of someone else. Details of the photograph provided the time clues: the man's tie, the lapels on his coat, his boots - even the furniture and the draperies in the room - all indicate the tintype photograph was taken after 1870 - six years after the *Hunley* sank - and perhaps even as late as 1890. This conclusion was reached by Jonathan Leader, a state archaeologist with the South Carolina Institute of Archaeology and Anthropology, who did research on the photo.

By the first part of December, work had been finished on the sub's central compartment. Investigation of the forward and aft ballast tanks was still not complete.

An exciting find was made in the last few days of the excavation in the area beneath the forward conning tower. The sub's depth gage was found but it was broken. Two pieces of approximately ¼ inch diameter glass tubes were found concreted to the submarine's hull near where Lt. Dixon's remains had been found. These tubes originally were filled with mercury and made up the manometer which was used to measure how far under the surface the sub was.

Activities in the year, 2002

Intensive work continued on the material previously recovered.

In June, 2002, the gold pocket watch of Dixon was recovered. The watch was found in a block of sediment holding some of Dixon's remains and appeared to be intact. The watch was not opened until 2003.

The scientists and genealogists were also beginning to unravel the story about the individual members of the *Hunley* crew. They had been studying the human remains found in the sub and trying to learn everything they could about each crew member's life story. As we have seen, only eight bodies were found on the submarine when stories of the sub had said, wrongly, that there were nine crewmen. The men ranged in age from about 19 to their early 40's. The final step in the work will be for the scientists to reconstruct the facial features of each person. The following scientists from the Smithsonian Institution will work on the remains: Dr. Doug

Owsley, head anthropologist at the Smithsonian, research assistant Rebecca Kardash, and Dr. Robert Mann, a hand and foot bone expert. Much of the work will center on artifacts that contain human remains such as shoes and textiles. Eight pairs of leather shoes have been found and all the shoes contain bones.

While work was being done on the sub in the Lasch Center, work also continued at the *Hunley* wreck site. In August, 2002, divers investigating the site made an unusual find. They found and recovered a three foot long iron piece with five points on it. It was not clear if the piece was a grappling hook used by the Federal navy looking for the *Hunley* or the anchor from the *Hunley* itself. The hook, covered with marine growth, was actually in the right place to be the anchor of the *Hunley*. It was 18 feet straight off the bow and was pointed back at the sub. The recovered hook is being stored in fresh water in the Lasch Center and its use is still being studied.

Also, in August, 2002, the scientists found that the femur bone from Lt. Dixon's left leg has a severe dent in it. They think that the dent was made when a bullet hit the $20.00 gold coin in Dixon's pocket during the battle of Shiloh. They believe that if the coin had not slowed and deflected the bullet Dixon would have been crippled or killed. The coin itself had been recovered from the sub in 2001. Since the coin's recovery, it was investigated by scientists with the South Carolina State Law Enforcement Division. They determined that the black marks on the coin are lead streaks. This supports the romantic story of the coin since Civil War bullets were made of lead

---

In October, 2002, *Hunley* officials announced they are looking at other methods of preserving the submarine besides the use of electrolysis that is now planned. The basic problem is the removal of corrosive salts that are now on and in the surface of the metal submarine. These salts, if not removed, will eventually destroy the submarine if it is exposed to the air and left untreated. Electrolysis makes use of passing electrical current through the submarine while it remains submerged in fresh water. A major problem with the electrolysis method is that the time of treatment will be about seven years. Another problem is that the method does not work efficiently behind bolted or riveted pieces. *Hunley* scientists are looking at two other methods that may be used and would cut the treatment time dramatically. They will test these methods on pieces from the boiler of a paddle steamer that sank off the coast of Australia in 1880.

The first method uses super and sub-critical water to remove the corrosive salts. Super and sub-critical water results when it is subjected to intense heat and pressure and acquires some unusual properties. One of these is the ability to quickly dissolve other materials.

The second method is cold plasma technology. In this method, hydrogen would be blown over the *Hunley* in a sealed container and the plasma formed would remove the impurities as a gas.

Both methods are being tested. If either method works on the *Hunley,* the treatment time could be shortened to a matter of hours instead of years. A major drawback to either method is that a large and strong pressure vessel would be needed to treat the entire sub. Otherwise, the sub would have to be taken apart and treated in smaller pressure vessels.

In November, 2002, recovery efforts presented more surprises as two pieces of diamond jewelry that were in the possession of Lt. George Dixon were found. One piece was a gold pinky ring with nine diamonds and the other a gold brooch with 37 diamonds. It is not known if the jewelry was for a man or woman. The estimated price for the ring today is about $1,500 re-tail and the brooch about $3,000. This does not reflect the price as valuable historic relics. This find is unusual for a fighting ship and they added yet another mystery to the *Hunley.*

The gold coin found on Lt. George Dixon went on display to the public in November, 2002. The coin can now be seen as part of the regular *Hunley* weekend tours.

Activities in the year, 2003

Intensive work continued on the material previously recovered and new discoveries were made.

A 3-by-5-inch leather wallet was found on the submarine in February, 2003, and many hoped it would hold clues of a sailor's personal life. However, when scientists opened the wallet, no contents were found.

The gold pocket watch belonging to Lt. Dixon was opened by the scientists in March, 2003. It was found to be stopped between 6 and 9 o'clock, but scientists warn that doesn't mean much in pinpointing the time the sub went down. The watch might have continued to tick for hours after Dixon and the rest of the crew succumbed to their fate, either by suffocating or drowning inside the submarine. Even though the sub sailed at night, scientists don't know if the watch stopped during the a.m. or p.m.

Hunley scientists opened Dixon's watch hoping it would reveal additional clues into the sub's final mission. The watch does not appear to contain trapped air. Inspection of the watchcase revealed that the interior latch that holds the case shut has corroded, and left the cover unsealed. It is decorated on both sides and includes a chain and an ornate fob, both made of gold. The chain of the watch was intertwined with very fragile, waterlogged textiles, meaning Lt. Dixon probably kept the watch in the pocket of a vest or coat.

The hour hand is broken at the stem. The only certainty is that the minute hand points to 22 minutes after the hour, and the second hand points to 20. The hands are very damaged and are fused to the watch face.

At some time in the future, the scientists will open the back portion of the watch where they hope to find an inscription giving more information. Several markings stamped into the gold on the outside could help determine who built the watch and where it came from. A purchase point might help the *Hunley* team find out more about Dixon, who was 26 years old when he commanded the sub. Not much more is known about him. The stamps include a lion, a horse's head that resembles a knight piece from a game of chess, a crown with the number 18 nearby - meaning it is 18 karat gold and serial numbers. The numbers on the watch face are Roman numerals. The watch is of the highest quality for the time, officials said, and efforts to find another one like it have proved fruitless.

In October, work began to excavate the ballast tanks on each end of the sub. Each tank was completely filled with sediment. During the first week of work, an unexpected find was made in the forward tank. A small, wooden cask about ten inches long and eight inches in diameter was found. The cask held a small amount of an orange colored substance. It was believed, at first, that the cask was part of some sort of mechanism use to measure the depth of water in the tank. However, further examination changed this idea. It now appears that the cask held a lead based material that was used to repair, or caulk, leaks in the seams of the sub's bulkheads and tanks. A small chisel, similar to a caulking iron, was found close to the cask.

The aft tank also had another artifact. A coil of rope was found there and carefully removed.

At the same time the tanks were being excavated, the crew compartment was being explored in more detail. Some of the items that were covered in heavy concretions were x-rayed and a wrench, a hammer and three bolts were identified. Another artillery uniform button was also found.

By the end of November, both tanks had been excavated. The empty ballast tanks and the excavated crew compartment will be given a digital, laser scan to accurately locate and measure all the components. The major components of the crew compartment such as crankshaft, crew bench, pumps, etc. will be taken out of the sub so that they can be thoroughly studied and conserved.

Efforts began for the reconstruction of the facial features of the crew. Forensic artist Sharon Long, assisted by physical anthropologist Dr. Douglas Owsley, worked with the information from the recovered remains to do facial reconstructions of each person. This work was completed in April, 2004.

Legacy of the *Hunley*. The submarine tender *USS Hunley* (AS31) docked with 10 modern submarines.
(US Navy Photograph)

Differences

Chapter 9

The actual submarine is different in many respects from what historians thought it would be. Before the recovery, the image of the *Hunley* was established by Civil War paintings, sketches and personal memories. The most important visual image of these sources was a painting by the famous Civil War artist Conrad Wise Chapman. This painting shows the *Hunley*, removed from the water, and sitting on a dock. This painting does not adequately reflect the true streamlined appearance of the sub.

The most detailed written description of the sub was an account by a former crewman, Mr. W.A. Alexander. He wrote his story for a New Orleans newspaper in 1902, over 37 years after the War. He gave information about the size of the submarine. We know now that Mr. Alexander remembered the *Hunley* as being larger than it really is. He described the inside of the crew area as four feet wide and five feet high. In actuality, the height of the sub, inside, was only about 48 inches and the width even less.

As the preservation effort continues, more information will be found about the *Hunley* and probably more differences between historical accounts and the actual sub will be found.

So far, the following differences have been found between the real submarine and previous concepts about it.

It has long been thought that the submarine had a crew of nine men. Mr. Alexander gave this number in his story. However, it appears that all of the human remains have been removed and only eight men have been found.

The sub is much more streamlined. Mr. Alexander said that the builders had taken a cylindrical locomotive boiler and added wedge shaped buoyancy tanks to each end. The replicas were built like this. However, the real sub builders had added tanks that were much more dagger shaped and curved. This gives the submarine a graceful, streamlined appearance that almost looks like a living thing.

As previously mentioned, the crew space was much smaller than believed. The average man, today, is several inches taller than the average man of the Civil War era. A large man could not have gotten into the sub. Crew members had to be small men and even they had to crouch severely to get into the sub and crank it.

The torpedo boom or spar was not mounted on the top of the sub. It was attached towards the bottom of the bow on a hinge type device that allowed the spar to be moved up and down. The recovered spar is made of iron, not wood, as believed before.

One very visible difference is that the sub's rivets are not as prominent as expected. The sub was made from a former locomotive boiler where large rivets with exposed heads are the rule. However, few rivets can be easily seen on the submarine. Some of the rivet heads are flat and are countersunk into the steel plates to lessen water resistance. The same method is still used in much aircraft construction. Further investigation of the sub will be required to see exactly how all the rivets are installed.

There are some small glass ports along the top of the submarine that allowed light to enter the boat. No prior mention had ever been found of this feature. Detailed investigation showed that these were sandwiched in place by inner and outer iron rings riveted and bolted.

There is a small rectangular glass view port in the front of the forward conning tower that allows the sub commander to see where he is going. It was known that there were viewing ports on the sides of the towers but not the front.

There are small pieces of iron installed on the sides of the sub that were evidently used for trim tabs to help stabilize the sub as it was being cranked.

It was thought that eight men actually cranked the boat - This is not true. There are only seven crank stations. Evidently, the ship's officer stationed in the stern of the sub performed other duties and did not operate the crank. It is possible, that at one time, the sub was fitted with eight cranking stations but was later modified. Mr. Alexander, in his story, describes how he and Dixon, at opposite ends of the boat, cranked at the same time. His sketches also show eight cranking stations.

The crew was thought to be positioned on both sides of the crank - This is also wrong. All of the men sat on the left side of the boat. Means were provided to offset their weight either by the weight of the crank support brackets or by another method not yet known.

New, unexpected features of the vessel have also been discovered:

A bellows has been found that is connected to the piping of the air box. This helped force air into the boat and made the air box more efficient than natural air flow. Evidence was also found that the air from the bellows may have been distributed to the crew members that were sitting further away.

The propeller driving system has been found to be more complex than originally thought. It was believed that the crank was fastened directly to the propeller. However, the drive has been found to have a set of sprocket gears, driving chain and a flywheel.

Another unexpected feature had to do with steering the sub. It was previously thought that Dixon steered the sub with a wheel mounted over his head. This wheel was believed to be connected to the rudder with rods or cables that ran in the overhead of the sub. This has been found not to be true. A vertical steering rod approximately 28 inches long has been found in the front end of the sub. The vertical steering rod could move in two directions from port to starboard for steering the sub. It appears that this rod is hinged at its base to a connection device that that runs through a pipe along the interior port side of the submarine underneath the crew bench to the stern area. In the stern, the connection would exit the submarine at some point and attach to the rudder, although further research still needs to be done to document exactly how all of this was interlinked.

One very important detail about operating the sub was also discovered. It was found that the forward and aft ballast tanks were connected by a pipe that ran under the crew's feet. This meant that water could be easily moved back and forth between the tanks making it much faster and simpler to trim the sub to dive, rise to the surface or stay level. No mention of this feature had been made in the contemporary accounts of the submarine.

Controversies about the *Hunley*

Chapter 10

Past Controversies

The submarine *Hunley* has been surrounded with controversy ever since it was built.

Some of the controversies from the past have been:

---

a. Who would be in charge and operate the submarine?

It was built in Mobile, Alabama and brought to Charleston by train. A civilian crew from Mobile came along and first operated the boat. Some officers in the Confederate army thought they were timid in not attacking the Federal fleet right away. The Confederate Government took control of the ship and replaced the civilians with a military crew.

---

b. Should it attack while submerged or stay on the surface?

The boat was built to surface and submerge as a real submarine. After the disastrous sinking while diving under the vessel *Indian Chief*, General Beauregard ordered it to only operate on the surface. Many associated with the *Hunley* wanted to operate as a true submarine.

---

c. Ever since the sinking in 1864, historians have been in disagreement about many things related to the submarine. Some of these are still not settled, such as:
How many times did it sink ?
How many crewmen died in its operation?

---

d. What kind of torpedo was used?

There was a dispute about the torpedo used by *the Hunley*. Some said it had a barb and was stuck into the enemy ship and detonated by a rope after it had backed away. Others said the torpedo was mounted on a long wooden pole and detonated by contact fuses when pushed against the enemy ship. (This was the view of Milby Burton, the historian/director of the Charleston Museum when the replica there was built.) Still others say the torpedo did blow up on contact but was mounted on a long iron rod that angled down so that it would hit the enemy ship below the water line. The recovery of the *Hunley* has provided a partial answer to this question. The torpedo was indeed mounted on a long iron rod or spar. But it did not necessarily angle down. The spar was mounted close to the bottom of the boat and could be adjusted up or down. Evidence now suggests that a barbed torpedo, detonated by pulling a rope, was used to sink the *Housatonic*. Another controversy about the torpedo is the amount of gunpowder it contained. Some accounts say 90 pounds, others say 135 pounds.

Modern Controversies

The controversy over the *Hunley* continues to this day. The recent discovery and recovery of the boat has resulted in major disputes that the original crew of the boat could not have imagined. Some of these are:

---

a. Who owned the wreck of the Hunley?

This has been resolved by an agreement where the Federal Government owns the vessel but it is in permanent custody of South Carolina.

---

b. Did Clive Cussler and his organization find the Hunley by themselves?

A researcher, working with the University of South Carolina Institute of Archeology and Anthropology, claims that he was working with Cussler and his group when Cussler violated the agreement and claimed finding the *Hunley* for himself and his divers. Cussler complained in the press about the researchers future involvement with the submarine. Because of the controversy, the University of South Carolina removed the researcher from the *Hunley* pro-

ject in June of 1995. The researcher then resigned from his job with the University.

---

c. Had the Hunley been found previously?

A Charleston diver has claimed that he found the lost submarine in 1970. Although he never offered any proof, the diver filed Federal papers claiming the *Hunley* find. In September, 1995, the diver signed any claim he might have on the *Hunley* over to the state of South Carolina. Shortly after this, officials from the South Carolina Institute of Archeology and Anthropology asked this diver to help them find the wreck. This was during the five months period in 1995 between Cussler's announcement that the boat was found and his release of the sub's exact position.

---

d. In what state should the raised and preserved Hunley be permanently displayed?

When the sub was found, both South Carolina and Alabama officials wanted it to be put on permanent display in their states. Alabama's claim was based on the fact that the boat was built in Mobile before being brought to Charleston. Some members of the Alabama Congressional delegation included a report in the Defense Appropriations Act saying the *Hunley* should go to Alabama. South Carolina Senator Fritz Hollings took measures to block the language of that request. South Carolina Congressman Mark Sanford introduced a bill that would convey Federal ownership to South Carolina. As said previously, this controversy was resolved with the boat coming to South Carolina but still owned by the USA.

---

e. Where should the submarine be placed while the restoration process is being done?

Original plans called for the *Hunley* to be put on display at a new section of the Charleston Museum. However, when funding for the new section was slow in coming, an effort was started by the *Hunley* Commission to investigate having the submarine placed on the former Naval Shipyard while it was being restored and put into condition for display. In addition, other sites besides the Charleston Museum would be considered for permanent display. This effort was strongly resisted by the City of Charleston officials, including Mayor Joe Riley. They were concerned that the move might become permanent and the *Hunley* would never be returned to the Museum. As a result of this controversy, money has been approved for the new *Hunley* wing of the Charleston Museum and architectural and construction plans are underway. However, since that time, the wisdom of this plan has been seen by all of the parties involved. There are special considerations for the area to be used for restoration that can be done cheaper at the former shipyard than at the Museum. There will be tons of silt and water to cope with during restoration that will not be necessary for permanent display. The restoration process may take as long as seven years. Public viewing of the sub will be possible during the restoration.

---

f. Should the Hunley have been recovered at all or left as a memorial to the crew?

Since it was found, there were definite plans underway to raise and restore the boat. However, there is a vocal minority that feel strongly that the boat should have been left in place and undisturbed. These sentiments were often seen in letters to the Editor of the *Charleston Post and Courier* newspaper.

Biggest Controversy

Possibly the biggest controversy about the *Hunley* concerned the location of the future, permanent home of the submarine. Three Charleston area communities were competing to be the location for the *Hunley* museum. The *Hunley* is expected to bring tourists from all over the world to Charleston. The cities of Charleston, North Charleston and Mount Pleasant made proposals to the *Hunley* Commission about how they would support and display the *Hunley* when preservation efforts are completed. The time of preservation may be much less than the original estimate of seven years because of the potential of a new method of preservation. The summary of each city's proposal was as follows:

City of Charleston

The city of Charleston proposed the Hunley Museum be built on Liberty Square between the new National Park Service Fort Sumter Visitors Center and the Dockside Condominiums. The site is very close to the spot where the Hunley was first put into Charleston harbor in 1863. The site also has a view of Fort Sumter and Charleston Harbor. The city said the Hunley site would benefit from being in the area now visited by thousands of tourists.

City of North Charleston

North Charleston proposed to permanently house the recovered vessel on a Cooper River site adjoining the northern end of the former Charleston Navy Base.

This is an 11 acre site near Lusch laboratory where the H dergoing preservation. This wo of the planned 20-year, 3,000-acre, $1 billion Noisette project to revitalize North Charleston.

City of Mount Pleasant

The city proposed to display the Hunley at the Patriot's Point Naval and Maritime Museum. This is the Naval and Maritime Museum for South Carolina. The Hunley would be a centerpiece for one of the most successful museums of its kind in the United States, with its own facility, designed specifically for its unique exhibition. Patriot's Point already has over 400,000 visitors per year.

These proposals were submitted in the spring of 2001 and a decision was expected sometime later that year. However the South Carolina *Hunley* Commission had concerns about the financial portion of each proposal and asked for additional information. In December, 2002, the Commission announced that the decision had been postponed indefinitely. Finally, in February, 2004, the *Hunley* Commission announced that the city of North Charleston had been chosen to become the permanent home of the submarine.

he Charleston Museum and The *Hunley*

Chapter 11

The Charleston Museum help keep the memory of the *Hunley* alive for much of the time the submarine was lost. Because the *Hunley* played such an important role in Charleston's history, a group of local citizens decided to build a replica of this historic submarine so that its story was not forgotten. The group included E. Milby Burton, then Director of the Charleston Museum and representatives of the Citizens and Southern National Bank.

In September of 1966, this group contacted Charleston Technical Education Center (now Trident Technical College) to see if they would build the replica.

The school director, Captain Howard Hoffberg, accepted the project as a public service. The design of the boat was assigned to the Mechanical Engineering Technology Department. At that time, the author of this book was the head of that department. This book is the result of his children's interest in the *Hunley* replica.

The most difficult part of the job was finding out exactly what the original *Hunley* was like. Several accounts written during the Civil War mentioned the *Hunley*. Most of these were vague and often contradictory.

The most reliable source seemed to be a painting by the Confederate artist Conrad Wise Chapman. This had been used by Mr. Floyd D. Houston to construct a small scale model of the *Hunley* for the Charleston Museum. This model was on a scale of 1/2 inch equals a foot. It was decided to use this model as the basis for the full size replica.

The Mechanical Engineering students measured this model very carefully. They then converted the measurements into complete engineering drawings that could actually be used in construction. The finished boat had to have a realistic appearance and be readily manufactured in the school's shops.

It was decided to use a completely welded structure with the caulking and rivets of the Civil War simulated to look like the real thing. Each feature of the replica was designed and drawn as close as possible to the original. When the Mechanical Engineering class was finished, they had a construction package containing 40 engineering drawings of assemblies and details.

This set of drawings was given to the TEC welding and machine shops where the actual construction was done under the direction of Mr. Clay Cabiness.

Upon completion of sandblasting and painting, the submarine was ready to move. The project started in October, 1966 and was finished in June, 1967. A house moving company was commissioned to do the moving and installation. Charlestonians were surprised to see an antique submarine going down its main streets. The submarine was taken first to the Charleston Navy Yard where pictures were made comparing it to present day submarines.

The first home of the *Hunley* replica was the basement of the Citizens and Southern National Bank on Church Street. However, after serving as a branch of the museum for several years, the building was destined for other uses. The *Hunley* was moved to become a prominent display for the Charleston Museum on Meeting Street. The replica has indeed helped keep the story of the *Hunley* alive to many Charlestonians and tourists

As pointed out elsewhere in this book, there are a number of differences between the recovered sub and the replica. This replica has been much in the news since the real *Hunley* was found. Pictures of the replica were often used to illustrate news stories about the discovery. The divers that found the real sub visited the replica that same night to discuss the differences between what they had found and the replica.

The story of the *Hunley* described in this book, before its recovery, is based on reference material furnished by the Charleston Museum when the replica was built.

Replica on display outside Charleston Museum.

Perspective
The *Hunley* Comes Home

Chapter 12

When they closed the hatches on the *Hunley* that cold February night, the end of the Civil War was over a year away. It was not certain, by any means, which side was going to win. In February, 1864, the Federal western army was still in Chattanooga and Sherman was still in Mississippi. The campaign to take Atlanta had not started. Ulysses S. Grant was still about a month away from being named new General in Chief of the Federal army.

In Charleston, the Federal army and navy were still trying to capture the city but were having little success. The blockading fleet was slowly strangling the South. They were preventing more and more ships from entering and leaving Charleston and other southern ports.

The sole reason that the *Hunley* existed was to try to break that blockade. On that cold night on February 17, 1864, the little submarine and its eight man crew had its chance. After closing the hatches, the crew slowly cranked the little ship out of Breach Inlet towards the lights of the blockading fleet that could be seen off the Isle of Palms and Sullivan's Island.

The early light of dawn the next morning gave drastic testimony to the success of the *Hunley's* mission. The masts and part of the super structure of the blockading ship, *USS Housatonic* could be seen sticking up out of the water. The boat had been quickly sunk by the *Hunley's* exploding spar torpedo at its patrol station about three miles offshore from the Isle of Palms.

Five Federal sailors had met a violent death when the ship sank. Many of the survivors had climbed up into the ships rigging until they could be rescued.

The eight man crew of the *Hunley* were also victims of their own attack. The death toll on both ships was thirteen men. These were men who believed that they were serving their country and protecting their freedom. They all paid the supreme price for their part in history.

There were thirteen families that would not have a son or husband or brother or father return from the War. All of the northern families would eventually learn of about the death of their relative. This would be through contact with the War Department, newspapers or letters from fellow sailors who served with those that were killed. However, many of the *Hunley* crew member's families probably never knew what happened. They only knew that at the end of the terrible War, their relatives just never came home.

The Charleston and the United States that the *Hunley* crew left in 1864 is unbelievably different than that of today. They had not seen automobiles, telephones, airplanes or almost everything we now take for granted. In the 136 years they have been gone, the world changed probably beyond their wildest dreams.

The crew never knew it, but their little submarine had changed naval warfare forever. The descendants of the little sub would play a major role in World Wars I and II and help win the Cold War. The blockading fleet that the *Hunley* attacked was supported by a Federal navy base at Port Royal near Beaufort. After the War, the US moved this and built a big shipyard at Charleston itself. For 90 years, ships going to and from the Charleston Naval Shipyard passed close by where the *Hunley* lay on the shallow ocean bottom. There were many kinds of surface ships and bigger and bigger submarines. Some of the submarines were powered by nuclear reactors, a far cry from being hand cranked. Some carried sixteen missiles, each almost as big as the entire *Hunley* submarine. The Charleston Naval Shipyard eventually struck its own political torpedo and was closed in 1996 shortly after the *Hunley* was found.

Now the *Hunley* had come home. She had passed by Morris Island the site of the bloody attack on Fort Wagner. She passed by Fort Sumter where the terrible War had started and Fort Moultrie whose big guns had helped keep the Federal troops out of the City for almost four years. She passed close to the areas where two of her former crews had met tragic deaths. She passed close to the docks she had originally used when first unloaded from the two railway cars that had brought her from Mobile, Alabama.

She went slowly by the *USS Yorktown,* a bigger ship than any *Hunley* crewman could ever have imagined. On the deck high above the Cooper River, nine ladies were waiting. Each was dressed in the fashion of women in mourning in the Civil War era. Each was representing a family of a *Hunley* crewman, then thought to be nine men. As the submarine went slowly by, each lady dropped a wreath in the water in memory and honor of her adopted sailor. What the families were unable to do 136 years ago, the women, dressed in black, did on August 8th, 2000.

On up the Cooper River she came. Slowly passing Magnolia Cemetery, the final resting place of the other two crews that had also been drowned during the War. In April, 2004, there was a sad reunion when this final *Hunley* crew was also buried alongside both the crews resting in

Magnolia.

Finally, she came into the former Charleston Naval Shipyard. There, the remains of her crew were removed and the little sub preserved to tell its story for the future. Generations not yet born will learn about the submarine and its brave crews. They will learn of the bravery and sacrifice of those sailors on both sides, Blue and Grey, Confederates and Federals, Americans all.

Re-enactors from the 54th Massachusetts Regt. salute the *Hunley*.

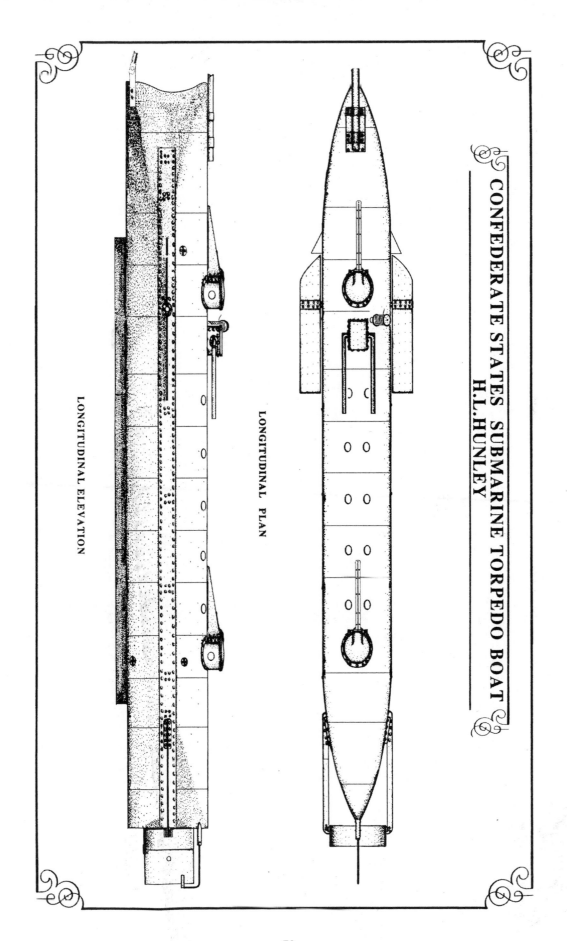

CONFEDERATE STATES SUBMARINE TORPEDO BOAT
H.L.HUNLEY

LONGITUDINAL ELEVATION

LONGITUDINAL PLAN

GLOSSARY

Part 1– The Submarine and Its Operation

Alexander, Lt. William A. - An officer and mechanical engineer in the State Artillery of the Twenty First Alabama Regiment. He assisted in building the *Hunley* at the Park and Lyons Machine shop. He was a member of the crew of the *Hunley* for a time. His memories of the *Hunley*, written after the war, seem to be the most complete description of the submarine available.

Back Bay - The term W. A. Alexander used for the area behind Battery Marshall at the end of Sullivan's Island.

Battery Marshall - Confederate fortification at the northern end of Sullivan's Island. It was located in the area next to Breach Inlet.

Beauregard, General Pierre Gustave Toutant - Confederate General from Louisiana. He was in command of the Military Operations in Charleston, including the attack on Fort Sumter that started the war. He left Charleston in early 1862 for the Western Campaigns. He was second in command to General A. S. Johnson at the battle of Shiloh in Tennessee. He later returned to Charleston for the second time and was in command of the *Hunley* operations. After the war he became a railroad president. He also became a Supervisor for the Louisiana Lottery.

Chain Booms - Devices similar to nets that were placed for protection around the Federal ships. The purpose of these booms was to keep Confederate torpedo boats from getting close enough to explode a torpedo against the hull. The Federal navy started to take major protection against torpedo attacks following the *David* attack against the *New Ironsides*.

Charleston, S. C. - The southern port city where the events in this book took place. Charleston was occupied by Federal forces on February 18, 1864 when it was evacuated by the Confederate forces. The approach of Sherman's troops by land made the city impossible to defend. After a siege of over two years, the city was taken.

David **-** A small Confederate steam torpedo boat. The *David* was built near Charleston, S.C. This little boat was used to attack the Federal ship *New Ironsides* on October 5, 1863. Several *David* type ships were built by the South during the war.

Dixon, Lt. George E. - A Confederate Army Officer and mechanical engineer in the Twenty-first Alabama Regiment. He, along with W. A. Alexander, was assigned to assist in building the *Hunley* at the Park and Lyons shop. Later he was given command of the *Hunley*. He was in charge and lost his life when it attacked the Housatonic. Lt. Dixon is the "Dixon" referred to by W. A. Alexander in his eyewitness account in Chapter 4.

Ebb Tide - The tide as it is receding or flowing back out to sea.

Fort Sumter - The fort situated at the mouth of Charleston Harbor. The first shot of the Civil War was fired at Federal troops in Fort Sumter on 12 April, 1861.

Housatonic - The Federal ship *U.S.S Housatonic*. One of the Federal ships on blockade duty. The *Housatonic* was a new steam sloop of war carrying eleven large guns. It was built at the Boston Navy Yard and had a crew of 145 men.

Hunley, Horace Lawson - A captain in the Confederate army who was largely responsible for building the submarine. He actually put up most of the money to build the ship. He was born in 1825 in Sumner County, Tenn. He moved to New Orleans as a child and later became a wealthy business man. His business career involved sugar cane planting, a law practice in New Orleans, and being a deputy customs collector for the port of New Orleans. He died in the submarine that bore his name during an accident in the Charleston harbor on October 15, 1863. He is buried in Magnolia Cemetery in Charleston, S. C.

Indian Chief - A Confederate ship stationed in Charleston Harbor. The *Hunley* was making a practice dive under the *Indian Chief* on October 15, 1863 when the submarine flooded and killed all aboard.

Ironsides - The Federal ship the *U.S.S. New Ironsides*. A powerful ironclad that was part of the blockading fleet. The *New Ironsides* had been attacked and damaged by the Confederate surface torpedo boat *David* on October 5, 1863. This attack alerted the Federal navy to the threat of torpedo attack and made the job of the *Hunley* more difficult.

Jordan, General Thomas - Confederate general who was Gen. Beauregard's Chief of Staff at both Charleston and Shiloh. He became a newspaper editor at Memphis, Tenn. He was a roommate of the Federal General Sherman during their cadet days at West Point.

Magnolia Cemetery - The city cemetery of Charleston. It is located on the Cooper River. Horace L. Hunley, Thomas W. Parks and the remainder of their crew are buried there. The eight members of the recovered *Hunley* crew will be buried there in 2004.

McClintock, Capt. James - One of the original designers and builders of the Confederate submarine. He was a partner with Baxter Watson in a steam gage and munitions company in New Orleans, LA. McClintock and Watson assisted Hunley in building the first two submarines. One submarine sank in Lake Pontchartrain and the other at Mobile, Alabama. McClintock and Watson's plans were used to help build the third submarine, the *Hunley*.

Monitor - A heavily armored ship that has one or more revolving gun turrets. It also usually sits very low in the water. There were several monitors with the Federal blockading fleet. The general term monitor should not be confused with the particular ship with that name that fought the *CSS Virginia (Merrimac)* in Virginia.

Naval Terms of Direction-
a.   Bow-The front end of the boat
b.   Forward-Toward the front of the boat
c.   Aft-Toward the back of the boat
d.   Stern-The rear end of the boat
e.   Port-Left side facing forward
f.   Starboard-Right side facing forward

Parks, Thomas W. - One of the co-owners of the Parks and Lyons Machine shop in Mobile where the *Hunley* was built. He was killed along with H. L. Hunley and the rest of the crew in the practice dive under the *Indian Chief*. He is buried in Magnolia Cemetery.

Payne, Lt. John - A lieutenant in the Confederate navy. He was the first military commander of the *Hunley* in Charleston. He survived the first accidental sinking of the *Hunley*. He was transferred from the *Hunley* and did not take part in the attack on the *Housatonic*.

Picket Boats - Boats or ships on guard duty. Term was used for Federal ships on blockade duty or for Confederate vessels on duty in the harbor.

Pilots - Men who in peacetime guided commercial ships into Charleston harbor. They were very familiar with the ship channels, tides, currents, and wind patterns. During the war, they were a great assistance to the Confederate navy.

Rains, General Gabriel James - Confederate General from North Carolina. He was an officer on General Beauregard's staff. He was named head of the Army Torpedo Bureau in June of 1864. He is given credit with the first use of land mines and booby traps in warfare during the Peninsula campaign in Virginia in 1861 and 1862.

Torpedo boat - Term used to describe any of the small boats used by the Confederacy that were armed with torpedoes. They varied greatly. Some like the *Torch* and the *David* were steam powered and operated on the surface. The *Hunley* was man-powered and could submerge. Efforts were even made to use torpedoes from row boats.

Wabash - The Federal ship *U.S.S. Wabash*. The *Wabash* had 44 guns and was the flagship of the Federal Admiral Samuel Francis Dupont. A business, John Fraiser and Company, offered a reward of $100,000 to anyone that could sink or destroy the *Wabash* or the *New Ironsides*.

Watson, Baxter - One of the original designers and builders of the Confederate submarine. (See McClintock)

Parts of the *Hunley*–

    a.   **Air Box** - This was a chamber on top of the submarine that was connected to a four foot length of 1½ in. pipe. This pipe could be rotated to point upward. After the pipe was pointed upward, a valve could be opened to allow air to enter the submarine. The valve was closed when the end of the pipe was underwater. The air box on the *Hunley* was a crude version of the snorkel that did not appear on modern submarines until World War II. The recovered sub revealed that the air box was fitted with a hand operated bellows that helped pull air into the boat.

    b.   **Ballast** - Pieces of cast iron that were located in a row along the underside of the submarine. The ballast made the submarine heavy enough to sink. Each piece of cast iron had a bolt going up into the submarine. In an emergency, the ballast could be dropped by turning these bolts. Changes to the submarine buoyancy for normal operations were made by using the ballast tank and not the cast iron ballast.

    c.   **Ballast Tank** - The submarine had two, one in front and one in the back. Each tank had a pipe and valve that allowed sea water to fill up the tank. The tank full of sea water made the submarine heavy enough to sink below the surface. When the crew was ready to come to the top, the tank could be emptied back into the ocean by means of a hand pump. The empty tank made the submarine lighter and it would float on the surface. Unfortunately, the tanks were open on the top. This meant that if the sea valves were not closed quickly enough, the tank would over-flow and let sea water fill up the inside of the submarine. Evidently, this is what happened when H. L. Hunley and his crew drowned.

    d.   **Boom** - The iron pole or spar that was attached to the lower part of the bow of the submarine. The torpedo was fitted to this spar, which is about 17 feet long.

    e.   **Crankshaft or crank** - The device that actually turned the submarine propeller. It was like a long pipe attached to the propeller. Seven men turned the crank which, in turn, rotated the propeller by way of a chain drive and flywheel.

    f.   **Diving Planes** - These were the flat pieces of metal sticking out on each side of the boat. They could be tilted from inside the boat to make the submarine go up or down.

    g.   **Hatch** - The opening in the submarine through which the crew entered. It had a watertight cover that could be fastened down before diving.

    h.   **Manometer** - A device used to measure pressure. In a submarine, the deeper you go underwater, the greater the pressure. Therefore, the manometer can also be used to measure the water depth. The manometer on the *Hunley* consisted of a "U" shaped glass tube filled with mercury. Mercury is about 13.5 times heavier than water. When the *Hunley* was 13.5 feet under water the mercury level in the manometer would be displaced one foot or 12 inches. The manometer tube could then be marked off or graduated, in the number of feet the submarine was below the surface.

    i.   **Rudder** - The rudder was a flat, vertical metal plate at the very stern of the submarine. The rudder steered the boat toward the left or right. The steering lever was up next to the forward ballast tank bulkhead. The submarine commander moved the lever which was connected back to the rudder by metal rods under the crew's bench and then through a stuffing box to the rudder.

j. **Stuffing Box** - A device that allowed an operating rod to pass through the submarine hull but did not allow water to enter. The stuffing box contained some sort of soft material like ropes or cloth. This material, or "stuffing", was pressed against the operating rod to seal out water. On the *Hunley* the stuffing boxes had bolts that could be tightened down to pack the stuffing.

k. **Torpedo** - A Civil War term for almost any type explosive device that was not shot from a gun. The torpedo that was attached to the *Hunley* boom was like a small keg packed with ninety pounds of black powder. The torpedo also had "fuses." These were small devices that would explode or give off a spark when struck or activated. This small explosion or spark would then make the black powder charge explode. There were also floating torpedoes or what we would call mines today. Some of the floating torpedoes exploded on contact. Others could be fired from shore by a electric wire that ran from shore and was attached to a battery. Others, like the one on the *Hunley*, could be activated by pulling a rope. This rope detonated the fuse which, in turn, ignited the powder in the torpedo. When the Federal Admiral Farragut said at Mobile Bay, "Damn the torpedoes, full speed ahead," he was talking about floating mines. What we today call a torpedo, that is shot from a submarine, was not developed until about the time of World War I.

Part 2 - Recovery and Restoration of the Submarine

Cussler, Clive - The best selling author who financed and led the successful efforts to find the *Hunley*. He is the founder and Chairman of the National Underwater Marine Agency (NUMA) an organization dedicated to locating lost shipwrecks.

Friends of the *Hunley* - A group created by the South Carolina *Hunley* Commission. Their mission is to raise funds for the recovery, conservation, and exhibition of the submarine. The members of the board of directors of the Friends of the *Hunley* are appointed by the *Hunley* Commission.

Hall, Wes - One of the divers, working for Clive Cussler, who actually helped find the *Hunley*.

***Hunley* Commission** - The organization created by the State of South Carolina to acquire, recover, and preserve the *H.L. Hunley*.

Jacobsen, Maria - Senior Archaeologist of the Friends of the *Hunley* project. She is from Texas A&M University and is leading the excavation of the interior of the submarine.

Karlissa B - The huge platform crane used as the base of operations for the *Hunley* recovery and actually used to lift the submarine from the bottom.

Lasch, Warren - The Chairman of the Friends of the *Hunley* organization. He is a businessman, fund raiser, and financial contributor to the *Hunley* effort. The laboratory where the sub is being examined and preserved is named for him.

Marks Tide - The 180 foot long work boat used in the initial part of the recovery efforts for the *Hunley*.

Mardikian, Paul - Senior Conservator of the Friends of the *Hunley* project. He is from the Sorbonne University Conservation Program in Paris and will be in charge of the conservation of the sub and its contents.

McConnell, Glenn F. - South Carolina state Senator who has been instrumental in spearheading the entire *Hunley* project. He is the Chairman of the *Hunley* Commission.

National Underwater Marine Agency (NUMA) - An organization founded by Clive Cussler dedicated to finding shipwrecks. It has located over 60 lost wreck sites. Locating the *Hunley* was a NUMA project.

Neyland, Dr. Robert - *Hunley* Project Manager and Chief Archaeologist for the Friends of the *Hunley*. He is normally the Branch Head of Underwater Archaeology for the Naval Historical Center but is on loan from the Navy to head the *Hunley* project.

Oceaneering International, Inc. - The company that was hired to plan the recovery and raise the *Hunley*. They were hugely successful in this very delicate, and potentially disastrous, operation.

Pecorelli, Harry - One of the divers, working for Clive Cussler, who actually helped find the *Hunley*.

Warren Lasch Conservation Center - The laboratory where the investigation and preservation of the *Hunley* is taking place. The building was a part of the former Charleston Naval Shipyard. It has been equipped and outfitted to be one of the most advanced maritime conservation laboratories in the world.

Wilbanks, Ralph - One of the divers, working for Clive Cussler, who actually helped find the *Hunley*.

About the Author

Gerald F. Teaster is a graduate Mechanical Engineer and a licensed Professional Engineer. He has worked in private industry, technical education and with the U.S. Department of Defense. Twenty one years of this was for the US Navy working on modern submarines and other ships. He was also the Chairman of the Engineering Technology Division and Department Head for Mechanical Engineering Technology at what is now Trident Technical College in Charleston, SC. While there, the school was asked to make life size replicas of the Confederate submarine *Hunley* and the Confederate torpedo boat *David.* He led the effort to research and develop construction drawings for these projects. His involvement with these replicas led to the publication of his book, *The Confederate Submarine, H.L. Hunley*, published in 1989. The recovery of the *Hunley* in August, 2000 resulted in much new information about the submarine and its crew and prompted the writing of *Confederates Courageous.*